Titoism and Dissidence
Studies in the History and Dissolution of Communist Yugoslavia

Europäisches Forum

Bd./Vol. 11

PETER LANG
Frankfurt am Main · Berlin · Bern · New York · Paris · Wien

Tomislav Sunic

Titoism and Dissidence

Studies in the History and Dissolution of Communist Yugoslavia

PETER LANG
Europäischer Verlag der Wissenschaften

Die Deutsche Bibliothek - CIP-Einheitsaufnahme

Sunic, Tomislav:

Titoism and dissidence : studies in the history and dissolution of Communist Yugoslavia / Tomislav Sunic. - Frankfurt am Main ; Berlin ; Bern ; New York ; Paris ; Wien : Lang, 1995
(Europäisches Forum ; Bd. 11)
ISBN 3-631-47778-3

NE: GT

This volume was supervised
by Prof. Dr. Klaus Hornung

ISSN 0721-3018
ISBN 3-631-47778-3

Preface

The series *Europäisches Forum* started in 1981 with the study of Alexander Shtromas "Political Change and Social Development: The Case of the Soviet Union". Professor Shtromas' competent analysis proved to be a brilliant prognosis of the forthcoming historical events since the end of the 1980's. It examined the proper roots of M. Gorbachev's "perestroika" and the following revolutionary changes in Eastern Europe and the Soviet Union. This first volume of our series got international acknowledgement and went into a second printing in 1989. Thus, from the beginning, the project of the *Europäisches Forum* underlined the conviction that the term "Europe" cannot only be confined to Europe west of the former Iron Curtain, but must be extended to the whole of Europe.

The present studies of Tomislav Sunic (Ph.D. Santa Barbara 1988), as volume 11 of *Europäisches Forum* are now stepping into these traces. Dr. Sunic, born 1953 in Zagreb, is an internationally esteemed political scientist who lived, studied and taught in the United States for over a decade. In 1992 he returned to his native country as an official adviser to the Croatian government.

This volume examines the contemporary history of ex-Yugoslavia; the "first" Yugoslavia under the Karadjordjevic dynasty from 1918 to 1941, as well as the "second" Communist Yugoslavia which lasted from 1945 to 1990. The author analyzes the formation of the Titoist system which from the beginning proved to be a totalitarian dictatorship in spite of many superficial judgements in the West about its alleged "liberal" nature. These false judgements had been shared by many intellectuals in Western countries in the 1950's, 1970's regarding the Titoist system, seen by many as a kind of prototype of the then broadly discussed "third way" between Western capitalism and "real socialism" of the Soviet type.

Hand in hand with the exposition of the political, ethnic, and ideological developments of Titoist Yugoslavia Dr. Sunic analyzes the parallel trends of dissidence in the communist version of this "jail of nations" which had been an artificial creation of the 1918/19 peacemakers from the very beginning. Also, communist Yugoslavia proved to be a superficially camouflaged Serbian hegemony over a flock of nations and national minorities to which even cultural autonomy was denied, let alone national and democratic self-determination.

This analysis gets its special value from first hand sources and monographs by "Yugoslav" authors published during the last decade in the United States, Great Britain, and France and also from publications in ex-Yugoslavia and Germany. Thus Dr. Sunic's studies are not only filling a gap in the German debate on "Yugoslavia", but also provide an important contribution to the international scientific discourse on the deeper causes of the catastrophic events in former Yugoslavia since 1991.

Professor Dr. Klaus Hornung | August 1994

Table of Contents

Preface of the Author

The Yugoslav Mythology: A Multicultural Pathology

One must agree with Georges Sorel, that political myths have a long and durable life. For seventy-four years the Yugoslav state drew its legitimacy from the spirit of Versailles and Yalta, as well as from the Serb-inspired pan-Slavic mythology. By carefully manipulating the history of their constituent peoples, while glorifying their own, Yugoslav leaders managed to convince the world that Yugoslavia was a "model multiethnic state." Many global-minded pundits in the West followed suit and made a nice career by preaching the virtues of the Yugoslav multiethnic pot. By tirelessly vaunting the Yugoslav model, scores of starry-eyed Western academics gave, both pedagogically and psychologically, additional legitimacy to artificial Yugoslavia. In 1991, faced with massive geopolitical tremors, stretching from Siberia to Spain, the Yugoslav mythology began cracking up, and with it, its multiethnic mystique. The sudden beginning of the democratization of Yugoslavia, led, naturally, to the abrupt end of Yugoslavia, whose bloody postscripta are yet to unfold.

Nothing seemed easier for the European Community and the United Nations than to describe the 1991 Serbian aggression against Croatia as a Serbo-Croat tribal war. At the beginning of the conflict, France, America, and the gallery of faceless UN mediators, shrugged off the Serbian territorial appetites by calling them the result of the ancient Serbo-Croat balkanesque feud. After all, why would big powers have to intervene in an area of Europe, which, according to their definition of international law, did not require a precise definition of the aggressor vs. the victim? The UN and European Community paralysis was seen by the Serbs as a green light to salvage Yugoslavia by force-even if that meant destroying it by force. As self-declared victims of hard times and soft former allies, the Serbs are angry today at France and America. These two countries offered them once Yugoslavia – only to strip them of it today. In retrospect, good guys appear to be those who define the international system, which in 1993, unlike in 1919 and 1945, does not well suit the Serbs. By detour, one could use Edward Carr's dictum that before we study history we must first study a historian – if we were to decide who to side with in the Balkans. In the latest spasm of their endless victimology, Serbs are heaping today their anger for the collapse of Yugoslavia on everybody: the Vatican, Muslims, the CIA, the IV Reich, and of course, on always available nearby Croats.

All the rest seems to be distant history now. In 1990, on the eve of Yugoslavia's break-up, the majority of Catholic Slovens and Croats favored the transformation of the centralized Serb-dominated Yugoslavia into a confederal state. Serbian communist leader Slobodan Milosevic flatly refused the idea of confederal Yugoslavia for fear that Serbia could lose its historic Yugoslav mandate which it had received in Versailles in 1919, and inherited in Potsdam in 1945. When in 1991 Slovens and Croats voted in defiance for the complete divorce from Yugoslavia, the Yugoslav Army launched a large-scale invasion against Slovenian and Croat "fascist separatists." As the war began to rage, so did the inflated word fascism become an expedient all-out metaphor of the Western media vernacular. It was hurled by everybody at everybody – and therefore, it hit nobody. The Serbs see themselves as fighting the just war against the resurgent fascist papal Croatia and Islamic fundamentalism. The Western media, by contrast, is portraying the Serb President Slobodan Milosevic as fascist butcher of the Balkans, bent on ethnic cleansing. Yet, old dogs cannot learn new tricks. Milosevic is still a communist *apparatchik* and the party he presides over is still euphemistically called the Socialist Party of Serbia.

Unquestionably, the roots of the present conflict, in what in the past tense used to be Yugoslavia, are grounded in recent history, which, by now, has turned into self-serving mythology. During World War II, Serbia suffered under fascism but, like all European countries, also experimented with fascism. Serbia had its share of killing and suffering just like Croatia, or for that matter any other country in Europe. World War II and post-war sufferings of Muslims, Albanians, ethnic Germans, and Hungarians at the hands of the Yugoslav communists still appear to evade the contemporary media comparisons. Serbia's less glorious World War II past was for years swept under the red carpet of oblivion, first by Yugoslav communist clerics and then by contemporary Serbian hagiographers.

Our post-modernity offers a curious type of historical narrative in which the metaphor has totally been devoured by mathematics. Small wonder, therefore, that the real warfare in Bosnia and Herzegovina has ceased by now to be the war of Serb-Croat-Muslim memories; it has turned into a surreal war for the respective number of war dead and endlessly increasing national trigonometries. Since 1945 Yugoslav politicians, the Serb Christian Orthodox Church, and a number of Serb intellectuals, have steadily inflated the Serbian World War II casualties which portray Serbs as victims of inborn Croatian and German fascism. The President of Croatia, the former Partisan general and historian, Franjo Tudjman, is intensely hated in Serbia because his World War II body counts fly in the face of the Serbian victimology. Before becoming President of Croatia, Tudjman tried to demolish

Serbian and communist historiography by deflating the number of Serbian World War II dead from the official 700,000 to a very modest 70,000. Predictably, his excursion into historicism regarding the Serbian mythical martyrdom unleashed Serbia's wrath. Faced with a sudden Croatian attack on her mythology, Serbia launched, in 1991, the military counter-attack against separatist Croatia. Political reality may change, but mythical surreality must remain untainted by any profanity.

To grasp the Serbian anger at Croatia and the West one should read the 19th century Serbian satirist Radoje Domanovic. Domanovic described the royal house in serbia as the site of endless Byzantine persecution complexes coupled with pan-Slavic zeal to convert Catholic and Muslim Slavs. Serbian royal hallucinations, stretching from the House of Karadjordjevic all the way down to the House of Milosevic, are still visible in Belgrade today. Every Serb is made to believe that a conspiratorial West, along with Islamic East, is plotting to enslave the Serb people.

The more secular European Community and the United Nations also border on the mythical melodrama. Their vicarious humanism manifests itself in occasional drops of culinary diplomacy, as well as in the presence of "peace-keeping forces," in a country torn by violent war. UN Samaritans lecture against Serbian ethnic cleansing, forgetting that ethnic cleansing is only the post-modern spin-off of *cujus regio ejus religio* for all countries in the making. Ethnic cleansing did not start with Milosevic and his likes; it began with communist Tito, who, either killed or expelled half a million ethnic Germans and Hungarians from early Yugoslavia. Tito only practiced in chorus the art with other East European communists, which resulted in the largest German *Völkerwanderung* in history; from the Balkans to the Baltics; from Königsberg to Karlovac. Forty years later his successor Milosevic miscalculated; he grotesquely followed Tito's suit; he grotesquely failed.

During the brief communist interregnum, Tito's Yugoslavia offered the foreign visitor bizarre features, which only the morbid and satirical painter, the 17th century Jacques Callot, could catch under his pen. On one of Callot's pictures, showing the Thirty years war in Europe, one sees a scene of boundless popular revelry, near a tree decorated with dozens of hung men. Similarly, the Titoist Yugoslavia could for years boast the largest number of nudist beaches in Europe, but also the largest prison population per capita in Eastern Europe. Just like in permissive Amsterdam, one could freely light up a *joint* in the center of Belgrade or Zagreb, but one could easily end up, for a minor 'political incorrectness,' in a real communist joint. The surreal Yugoslav conviviality allowed everybody everything – provided one did not touch the infallibility of the mythical Tito. For forty years, the Yugoslav communist vocabulary dubbed every Croat a "fascist", if he ventured to evoke his national ancestry. In Yugoslavia, as everywhere else in Eastern Europe, one could display national sentiments and unfurl his flag only behind closed family doors or in the open soccer field.

The up-to-date targets of the Serb rage are not just the proverbial Croat Nazis and Muslim fundamentalists. All other neighboring nations, ethnic groups, and minorities, are being put in the category of fascist world conspirators. Ironically, Croats and Serbs hate each other most, probably because they resemble each other most. Is it not true that racism is always directed at the other, who psychologically and morphologically always represents the travesty of the Same? One does not discriminate against beasts; one discriminates against his likes. Following the logic of the cursed Other, a great number of Serbs, both in Serbia and Bosnia, are deeply convinced that ethnic cleansing is a rightful way to pursue a noble struggle against Croatia's fascism and Muslim fundamentalism, for which all military means and tools are morally justifiable. Destruction of Croatian Catholic churches and Muslim mosques, killing of thousands of non-Serbs, bears witness to the never ending logic of the worse. Tomorrow, times may change and political constellations may also alter. Who will prevent tomorrow's Albanians or nearby Hungarians from similar mythical aggrandizements and ethnic cleansing of Serbs? Permanent peace has never meant much in Europe; it has always been seen by the Other as punitive peace. Alas, the European laws of the tragic are timeless, and their meaning lies only in the bowels of wild geese, or in the rhymes of the Greek chorus ...

The Serbian government does not share alone the blame for the carnage in the Balkans. Western governments, particularly the United States and France, preached for decades the "unity and integrity" of Yugoslavia, as if Yugoslavia could be held together by some French decree or the State Department *ukase*. The US State Department and its year-long chief *apparatchik* Lawrence Eagleburger's decades-long support of "Yugoslavia's integrity," gave a decent alibi to Serbia's war of aggression. Hybrid Yugoslavia and Czechoslovakia, two virulently anti-German countries, had entered geopolitically neatly into the NATO doctrine of 'double containment'; on the one hand they contained the red Bear in the East, on the other, they contained the mythical and unpredictable German in the West. Small wonder, therefore, that nobody in Washington and Quai d'Orsay was ecstatic with the sudden disintegration of Yugoslavia. As the supreme irony of history, this time around it is not the proverbial "ugly German" who is destroying the Versailles architecture. This time, the Versailles architecture is falling apart due to its surreal Potemkin-Hollywood-like facade. Woodrow Wilson and his progeny suffered a serious defeat in Europe.

The whole holy story in the Balkans has just begun to unravel. The Serbian leadership in Belgrade shows great concern for Serbs living in Croatia and Bosnia, but ignores the rights of the swelling tide of Albanians in its own house. Albanians in Serbia, similar to Palestinians, have perfectly learned the ancient wisdom, which Christian Europe had forgotten long time ago: demography is the continuation of politics by other more enjoyable means. Any cohabitation in the Balkans, any brand of federalism or 'power-sharing,' which Western pundits preach until their dying breath, is out of the question. Endless wars seem to be the only answer. At some point, some outsider from a distant galaxy may reassemble bits and pieces of the scattered Berlin wall and fence off different versions of the ethnic truth. Multiethnic countries are like prisons, in which citizen-inmates communicate with the Other, only after each is granted his own territorial imperative Crammed in one promiscuous cell, all hell breaks loose. Short of a giant mine fields separating Serbs and Croats today, or Poles and Russians tomorrow, Europe will be entering another chapter of the hundred years war. When different historical destinies clash, when different national mythologies collide, and when different geopolitical tectonic plates start rattling under Eurasia, then the myth of united Europe will sound like a titanic joke.

Today it is the turn of ex-Yugoslavs to live the violent beauty of their congested multiethnic laboratory. Tomorrow it may be the turn of multiracial Marseille, Frankfurt or Bruxelles. 1992 events in sunny Los Angeles have shown time and again that no paradigm, no academic model, no formula, and no single truth can have an answer for our multicultural future. The multicultural daydream functions nicely in soft, sunny, "cool," and consumer society; with first heavy clouds it spells chaos of unbelievable proportions. French philosopher Emile Cioran, was right when he wrote that if we knew what the future holds for us, we would immediately strangle our children.

* * * *

The preceding preface was first published in August 1993 in *Chronicles, a magazine of American Culture*. The intention of that essay was to give the American reader a graphic idea of the unfolding Balkan drama, which by 1993, had hit all the newspapers and news agencies around the world. The chapters that follow, were written ten years ago, in 1984 as my Masters thesis in political science at the University of California, Sacramento. At that time of course, I could not anticipate the scope of the Yugoslav drama which would begin with Serbian aggression against Croatia in 1991. I hope that the reader will find some details about the repressive Titoist apparatus helpful in grasping the present violence in the Balkans.

Unfortunately, Titoist Yugoslavia did not receive due attention by scholars when Tito was still alive. Had it received such attention, some of the present savagery might have been avoided.

I would like to express my gratitude to Mr. Tomislav Urban, a Croatian-American student and my present assistant. Tomislav had the patience to go over my "Sacramento writings" and make a few updates.

Zagreb/Croatia, March 1994

Chapter I: Introduction

Opening Remarks

The state of Yugoslavia emerged during the aftermath of World War I as a creation of the treaty makers in Versailles and Trianon. The inhabitants of the new state – who were descendents of people living previously in Austria, Hungary, Serbia and Turkey – always experienced difficulty in assessing the value of their Yugoslav affiliations. Yugoslavia represented in the minds of many of its citizens more a geographical concept than a viable political entity; consequently, many Yugoslavs suffered a national identity crisis. The process of amalgamating five different nations and a wide variety of ethnic groups into one nation-state, headed by Serbian monarchy, aroused strong feelings that one nation was benefiting from the state more than others. Feelings of being culturally and economically exploited were particularly strong among the Croats.

Despite the well-meaning intentions and proud efforts of many Yugoslav politicians, the centrifugal forces of nationalism eroded the fragile Yugoslav unity and finally dealt its death blow in the early years of World War II, when Yugoslavia was fragmented by the German invasion of Yugoslav territory and by Croatia declaring itself a separate, independent state. The Allied victory in World War II and the Yalta agreement reestablished Yugoslavia as a nation-state, but this time under communist rule. Even under the rule of Tito and the Yugoslav Communist Party, and despite initial successes after the war, Yugoslavia still remained troubled by nationalist sentiments. The issue in Yugoslavia was twofold: 1) How to organize the state in such a way that one nation does not pose a threat to another, and 2) how to create a democratic society in which different political views are respected.

Yugoslav dissidents assumed, that they knew the solutions to these problems. Some imagined that the best solution was to dismember the state of Yugoslavia altogether. Others assumed the opposite, and advocated an even more unitaristic and centralized Yugoslavia. The issue was further complicated by the fact that many dissidents viewed the future of southern Slavs from their own national or ethnic perspectives; consequently, their ideas did not include the future of all southern Slavic nations, but only the survival of their own.

Tito, the founder of communist Yugoslavia, understood the inherent shortcomings of Yugoslav dissidents. Tito's rise to power and his program of unification were facilitated by the existing fragmentation of the various nations of southern Slavs. Tito also greatly benefited from the Yalta agreement which stipulatd the partition of Europe into East and West. From a global perspective, it can be said that Titoism contributed to peace in Europe. But seen on the regional level, Tito's government did not only inherit the unresolved national question in Yugoslavia, but actually allowed the situation to regress to a level characterized by post-Versailles Yugoslavia.

Purpose and Scope of Study

The purpose of this book is to describe and analyze the phenomenon of Titoism within the framework of Yugoslav history. Titoism will be analyzed in terms of its ideology and in relation to the unique character of political dissidence found in Yugoslavia, for it is the thesis of this book that the rise of Titoism and its continuation can be attributed in large part to the nationalistic character of Yugoslav dissidence.

After providing a brief orientation about the geography, peoples and history of modern Yugoslavia, this book will examine the nationalistic character of dissidence in Yugoslavia. Next, there will be an introductory discussion of Tito, Titoism and Yugoslav totalitarianism and a general outline of the relationship between Yugoslav dissidence and Titoism. Examining this general relationship between Yugoslav dissidence and Titoism within the context of Yugoslav history will constitute the body of this book, which is divided into five chapters. Chapter II is concerned with Yugoslav dissidence and the rise of Titoism during World War II. Chapters III and IV discuss Yugoslav dissidence and its relation to the continuation of Titoism during the period following World War II up until the death of Tito in 1980. Chapter V examines the continuation of Titoism and dissidence after the death of Tito.

Modern Yugoslavia: Geography, History and Peoples

Yugoslavia, the "land of southern Slavs," dominated the central and northeastern regions of the Balkan Peninsula in southeastern Europe. The country's location had strategic significance because it controlled the most important land routes form Central and Western Europe to the Aegean Sea and the Turkish Straits. Likewise, it controlled the important land routes from Eastern Europe to the Adriatic Sea. Additionally, it also had control of a portion of the Danube River – the most important navigable water route from Central and Western Europe to the Black Sea – which flowed through northeastern Yugoslavia from Hungary to Romania.

Yugoslavia was the ninth largest country in Europe, with a total of 98,766 square miles of territory. It was divided into three distinct topographical regions:

1. The fertile Panonnian Plain, constituting a quarter of Yugoslavia's area, lies to the north of the rivers Sava and Danube, and accounted for the majority of the country's commercial agricultural production.

2. A thin littoral along the Adriatic Sea, Dalmatia, constituted a second region which is typically Mediterranean in climate and flora. The scenic Dalmatian coast – because of its pleasant climate and plethora of small, picturesque islands – was economically important to Yugoslavia's economy because it attracted large numbers of tourists from all over Europe.

3. Between the Panonnian Plain and the Adriatic Sea lies the rugged Balkan Massif, covering more than half of Yugoslavia's territory. Beginning in the northwest along the Austro-Italian border, the mountain chain fans out along the Adriatic coast all the way south to Albania and Greece. Earthquakes are common in this area.

These mountains constituted a natural defensive barrier on all sides of Yugoslavia, save the northeast frontier of the Panonnian Plain. Mineral, metal and timber exploitation, as well as sheep raising, are important economic activities in the mountains. Yugoslavia was rich in lignite, asbestos, iron, chromium and copper. It ranked among the world's leading producers of antimony, mercury and bauxite. One third of Yugoslavia's surface was covered with forests[1].

Historically, Yugoslavia came into existence as a state in 1918, shortly after World War I. Its mosaic of different peoples and ethnic groups, the most diverse in all of Europe, has always represented a serious obstacle to achieving national unity. No matter what the form of government, the national question persisted throughout its history.

Slavic peoples came into the area later called Yugoslavia during the 6th Century A.D. Croats were the first to establish a kingdom in the 8th century. After the termination of their dynasty, brought about by internal strife and the Crusaders, the Croats joined Hungary in the 12th century (1102) and, later, Austria. Until 1918 Croatia was a part of the Austro-Hungarian Empire; after its downfall, Croats jointly founded – together with Serbs and Slovens – a new state which in 1921 became Yugoslavia.

---

1 See *Encyclopaedia Britannica*, 15th Ed., s.v. "Yugoslavia," pp. 1100-1103.

Map 1 – Yugoslavia

Source: Historical Maps of Croatia, p. 22, Croatian Information Centre, Zagreb 1993

The two largest groups of people in Yugoslavia were Serbs and Croats. Serbs represented the largest nation with a population of eight million. About 600,000 Serbs lived in Croatia and over two million Serbs lived in Bosnia and Hercegovina. Croatia was the second largest nation in Yugoslavia in terms of population and territory. One million Croats also lived in Bosnia and Hercegovina, which they claim as historic parts of Croatia. These regions are disputed by Croats and Serbs. Two million Croats also live abroad and represent one of the largest diaspora in the world. Seventy percent of the Croats are Catholic and twenty percent are Muslim; the majority of Serbs belong to the Orthodox Church[2].

Like Croats, Serbs created a medieval kingdom which reached its zenith under Tsar Dušan in the 14th Century. After his death, Serbia fell under the domination of the Ottoman Empire and remained under Turkish rule for four centuries. Turkish rule greatly affected the ethnic composition of the Balkans. Many Slavs were converted to Islam, especially in Bosnia and Hercegovina. Except for Croatia and Slovenia, all other parts of Yugoslavia were under some form of direct or indirect control by the Turks. The Turkish presence significantly disrupted the southern Slavs from remaining closely tied to Western Europe and developing the foundations of democratic institutions.

It also created a rift between northern Slavs (Croats and Slovenes) and those of the south (Serbs and Montenegrins). The differences between Yugoslav nations were truly enormous; they varied considerably according to language, religion and customs.

Serbia and Montenegro were the first to revive their states after the decline of the Ottoman Empire, and after the Congress of Berlin in 1878 they became fully independent. During World War I, both Serbia and Montenegro sided with France and Russia; thus, after the Allied victory they exerted considerable influence on the Croats and Slovenes who had sided with Austria and Germany. The new royal Yugoslavia, founded under the auspicies of the Serbian Karadjordjevic dynasty and the Versailles Treaty makers, failed to resolve the national question, let alone promote democracy as the basis for intra-national dialogue. The royal court fostered the ethnic unity of Yugoslavia not through mutual consensus and understanding, but through arbitrary arrests, repression of non-Serbian nations and the almost exclusive favoring of Serbs in all spheres of social and cultural life. In the words of Dennison Rusinow:

---

2 Francis Eterovich, *Croatia: Land, People, Culture* (Toronto: University of Toronto Press, 1964).

Table 1 – Nationalities In Yugoslavia, 1971 Census

	SFRY	Bosnia & Herce-govina	Monte-negro	Croatia	Mace-donia	Slo-venia	Serbia: Total	Serbia: Kosovo	Serbia: Vojvo-dina
Number of Inhabitants (in thousands)									
TOTAL	20,523	3,746	530	4,426	1,647	1,727	8,447	1,244	1,953
Serbs	8,143	1,393	40	627	46	20	6,017	228	1,089
Croats	4,527	772	9	3,514	4	43	185	8	139
Moslems	1,730	1,483	70	19	1	3	154	26	3
Slovenes	1,678	4	1	32	1	1,624	16	"	5
Albanians	1,310	4	36	4	280	1	985	916	3
Macedonians	1,195	2	1	6	1,142	1	43	1	17
Montenegrins	509	13	356	10	3	2	125	32	36
Hungarians	477	1	"	36	"	10	430	"	424
"Yugoslavs"	273	44	11	84	3	7	124	1	47
Turks	128	1	"	"	109	"	18	12	"
Others	486	19	3	75	56	13	320	18	184
Unknown	67	10	3	19	2	3	30	2	6
Percentage Composition									
TOTAL	100.0	100.0	100.0	100.0	100.0	100.0	100.0	100.0	100.0
Serbs	39.7	37.2	7.5	14.2	2.8	1.2	71.2	18.3	55.8
Croats	22.1	20.6	1.7	79.4	0.2	2.4	2.2	0.6	7.1
Moslems	8.4	39.6	13.2	0.4	0.1	0.2	1.8	2.1	0.2
Slovenes	8.2	0.1	0.2	0.7	0.1	94.0	0.2	"	0.3
Albanians	6.4	0.1	6.8	0.1	17.0	0.1	11.7	73.6	0.2
Macedonians	5.8	0.1	0.2	0.2	69.3	0.1	0.5	0.1	0.9
Montenegrins	2.5	0.3	67.2	0.2	0.2	0.1	1.5	2.6	1.8
Hungarians	2.3	"	"	0.8	"	0.6	5.1	"	21.7
"Yugoslavs"	1.3	1.2	2.1	1.9	0.2	0.4	1.5	0.1	2.4
Turks	0.6	"	"	"	6.6	"	0.2	1.0	"
Others	2.4	0.5	0.6	1.7	3.4	0.7	3.8	1.4	9.4
Unknown	0.3	0.3	0.5	0.4	0.1	0.2	0.3	0.2	0.3

Source: Oskar Gruenwald; The Yugoslav Search for Man; p. 296.

The Croats, Slovens and other non-Serbs in the south as well as the north, the majority of the population, found themselves living in what was really a Greater Serbia with a Serbian King, a Serbian capital, Serbian ministers and Serbian domination of the army and bureaucracy[3]

Croats, increasingly alienated through the overrepresentation of Serbs in Yugoslavia, waited for the first opportunity to establish an independent state; they succeeded during World War II with the help of Nazi Germany, but their state lasted only four years. The vacuum created by the occupiers and various fascist bands was filled by a miniscule communist party and its leader, Tito. Having created his movement on the basis of multi-nationality, and supported by the Allies, Tito rose to power in Yugoslavia during the last year of the war and remained in power until his death in May of 1980.

Serbia was the nation with the most sentiment for Yugoslavia as a state, and by its number and influence, it also represented the true guarantor of statehood and, to a much lesser extent, of Titoist communism. Croats and Albanians were known for their lack of Yugoslav sentiment and often expressed opinions described by the Titoists as "separatism" and "chauvinism". The westernized and urbanized Croats perceived Serbia as an expansionist force threatening the Croatian language, culture, history and, eventually, their biological survival. Furthermore, they considered the republic of Bosnia and Hercegovina as a region "stolen" from Croatia, "grabbed" by Serbs in conjunction with communists. Serbs, on the other hand, claimed their ethnic rights; that is, their numerical superiority in the republic of Bosnia and Hercegovina.

Ethnic Albanians represented a true non-Slav minority in Yugoslavia, even though their number surpassed the number of recognized Slovenes, Macedonians and Montenegrins. Serbs and Albanians argued, and still argue over the province of Kosovo, densely populated by ethnic Albanians, but claimed by Serbia as a part of the medieval "Great Serbia". Thus, with obvious contradiction, Serbs reject Croatian historical rights to Bosnia and Hercegovina as "fascist" and "reactionary" but, in their turn, use similar historical arguments in their claim to Kosovo. In Titoist Yugoslavia it was socially desirable to endorse the Serbian cause against non-Slavs and "primitive" Albanians in Kosovo, yet it was not permitted to advocate the cause of Croats in regard to Bosnia and Hercegovina. Since Serbs, Croats and Albanians were the most important groups in regard to Yugoslavia's stability, they will be analyzed further in Chapter V.

---

3 Dennison Rusinow, *The Yugoslav Experiment: 1948-1974*. (Berkeley: University of California Press, 1977), forword p. xvii.

The term "dissident" comes from the Latin, dis-sidere, meaning "to sit apart." Ethymologically, the term is significantly different from the noun "dissenter" which was derived from the Latin word dis-sentire – "to feel apart". Today, both terms have converged into the same meaning and are used in the description of a person in strong disagreement with the state-sponsored ideology.

In 17th century Europe Presbyterians, Baptists and Quakers were referred to as dissidents. Later, when they acquired civil liberties themselves, others became dissenting scapegoats bound to inevitable persecution, banishment or death. This irony of history repeats itself as former dissenters often turn into persecutors, while at the same time they generate a new brand of dissenters. One need only recall the first dissenters who ignited the French Revolution or the October Revolution in Russia. When the initial bliss of the revolution is over, the dissenters become the victims of their dissenting ideals. Nicolas Berdyayev, the old Russian revolutionary who turned into an anti-communist and exiled dissident, once his dreams about a socialist reality became shattered, observes: "The revolution of which the dissenting intelligensia always dreamed has come to become the end of the intelligensia"[4]. This disturbing verity might serve as a good example to those who are reluctant to learn from recent history.

Today, the term dissident has acquired a somewhat diluted connotation and frequently stands for an intellectual or academic who, through non-violent political action, challenges the foundations of his society. The word dissident cannot be equated with the word 'opposition'. Dissidents do not represent a political party or movement; although, under favorable circumstances the former might develop into the latter. In Eastern Europe, dissidents who lived under communist regimes had little success in creating political parties or movements. Yet, dissidents in some nations were able to generate an organized opposition, as in Poland, and succeeded in bringing about social change.

In Titoist Yugoslavia the word dissident was virtually non-existent. If it was used occasionally in the party organs, then precautions were taken to place the word under quotation marks in order to downplay its political connotation. The use and abuse of language played an important role in Titoist vernacular. Terms like "totalitarianism," "democracy" and "human rights violations" were sometimes mentioned in Yugoslavia, but the Com-

---

4 Nicolas Berdyayev, *The Origins of Russian Communism* (London: Geoffrey Bles, 1948), p. 155.

munist party controlled the context of their use. A person in Western Europe might have described critics of Titoism as dissidents, but this would have been inappropriate in the Yugoslav press and would have been avoided. Dissidents were considered non-existent, both constitutionally and judicially, and were thought of as superfluous in "democratic" Yugoslavia: "Why should anyone dissent in a country which claimed *de jure* and *de facto* to be a paragon of democracy?

Titoists in Yugoslavia not only forbid anyone from becoming a dissident, but they also rejected the notion that something might conceivably be wrong with Titoism. If a dissident in Yugoslavia was confronted by the law he would be prosecuted as a common criminal under the penal code – whether or not he had been violent or non-violent in his dissenting activities – and had only a meager chance of being acquitted. A dissident might have criticized Titoism within the limits "guaranteed" by the constitution, but once targeted by the authorities, he would likely have been discredited as a fascist, a foreign agent or a "hostile element"; consequently, the penal code was the only standard for measuring his sentence (see Chapter V).

Despite occasional outbursts of criticism from individual dissidents, Titoists seldom perceived the criticism as a direct threat to the political stability of the regime. In order to avoid the danger of dissidents becoming an organized opposition, the authorities dealt directly with the roots of dissidence rather than its consequences. Thus, the Titoists were largely successful in reducing the volume and voice of Yugoslav dissidence.

Yugoslav dissidents reflected the multi-national character of their state. Although they may have shared the common goal of promoting social change in Yugoslavia, they nevertheless differed in their concepts of reform and their methods. The diverse national background of Yugoslav dissidents played an important role in their ideological orientation, a role which often eclipsed their anti-communist or anti-Titoist endeavors. Seen as a whole, Yugoslavia represented a mosaic of different peoples, nations and minorities, each with their own history, customs, and often language and religion: a diversity incomparable to any other state in Europe, except the Soviet Union. Some Yugoslav dissidents had the habit of calling Yugoslavia "the reduced Soviet Union," alluding to a country made up of fifteen different republics and over one hundred different ethnic groups. Even if Yugoslavia had been a parliamentary democracy, it would still have faced the problems of different kinds of nationalism and separatism. A considerable number of Yugoslav dissidents not only opposed Titoist communism, they also rejected the idea of Yugoslavia, itself, precisely in the same fashion that Tito once rejected the Soviet tutelage of Yugoslavia. To many Yugoslav dissidents, the state of Yugoslavia represented an artificial creation of the Versailles

Treaty, harmful to the national and historical strivings of its respective nations and exacerbated by Tito's totalitarianism.

In an ethnically homogeneous country, such as Poland, the role of political dissidence was more prominent and was far more likely to gain much larger support among its citizens. By contrast, Spain – which today has a parliamentary democracy in which its citizens in the last few years have enjoyed civil liberties guaranteed by the constitution – is still marred by various dissident groups whose claims are often based on ethnicity and less on political ideology. In order to fully understand the character of dissidence in Yugoslavia, it is important to first appreciate the full power of nationalism in Europe, itself:

> An even greater paradox is that nationalism remains a most powerful force precisely in that area of Europe where communism has been established – communism which was supposed to eliminate nationalism forever[5].

Titoists in Yugoslavia never attempted to solve the national question because they considered it a relic of the past and an offspring of "bourgeois mentality." After the war, they assumed that nationalism would simply fade away in favour of a classless society based on anational principles. Communist assumptions have not proven correct. Moreover, communist countries had increasingly rejected internationalism as one of the basic concepts of communist ideology and had often tended towards an independent "national" communism[6]. Decades after the Great October Revolution the center of communism was not only Moscow, but Belgrade, Tirana, and Beijing. National consciousness was difficult to supress and it appears to be more enduring than class-consciousness.

Tito, Titoism and Yugoslav Totalitarianism

Titoist communism did not emerge overnight in Yugoslavia after World War II. The founder of Titoism, Josip Broz Tito (1892-1980), took some time before he began differentiating himself from his former mentor, Joseph Stalin. Tito broke away from the Soviet Union in 1948 only after serious divergences had arisen between him and Stalin concerning Yugoslavi-

---

5 Franjo Tudjman, *Nationalism in Contemporary Europe* (New York: University of Columbia Press, 1982), p. 3.

6 Titoists endorsed Yugoslav nationalism but fervently rejected independent nationalism within Yugoslavia, i.e., Croatian and Albanian nationalism.

a's domestic and foreign policy. Titoism in Yugoslavia was characterized by the following traits:

1. In terms of foreign policy, Yugoslavia was an independent, non-aligned communist nation not subject to Soviet domination, maintaining cordial relations with the West.

2. Domestically, Yugoslavia, officially, decentralized its state apparatus, abandoned centralized economic planning, introduced worker's self-management and brought an end to collectivization in agriculture. According to the scheme of self-management, the autonomy of districts, regions and republics was equal to that of the state. In the economic sphere, separate working units, factories, industrial complexes and agricultural centers were autonomous and did not depend on the decisions of federal authorities. In practice, this took place only on the lower state level and was never fully implemented by the authorities.

3. Despite visible differences with other communist countries of Eastern Europe, Yugoslavia was still under the firm control of the Yugoslav Communist Party and Marxist ideology. Yugoslavia bore the dictatorial, totalitarian imprint of Josip Broz Tito.

This book deals mostly with the third component of Titoism because it best illuminates the reality of post-World War II Yugoslavia and the character of its founders.

Tito's death in May 1980 remains for many as mysterious as his spectacular career[7]. Beginning as a Croat peasant, he volunteered for the Austrian Army and fought against the Serbs during World War I. He was taken prisoner in Tsarist Russia and became an eyewitness to the October Revolution. He subsequently became a leader of the Yugoslav Communist Party and ended up, with help from the Allies, establishing a communist Yugoslavia after World War II. He then broke with the Soviet Union under the banner of "communism in one country" and created a non-aligned Yugoslavia. Josip Broz – alias, Walter; alias, Old Man, or simply Tito – became an indisputable legend during his own time not only for Yugoslavs, but also for many Westerners. At Tito's funeral, French President Giscard d'Estaing referred to him as "a great international leader." British Prime Minister Margret Thatcher called him a "great statesman." United Nations Secretary General Kurt Waldheim eulogized him as "a true hero – the last of the great figures of our time." In contrast, many Yugoslavs perceive him in a different light as "the butcher of Bleiburg", the architect of the Yugo-

---

7 Officially, Tito died on May 5, 1980. Funeral preperations were made in early February, 1980. Simultaneously, some Yugoslav newspapers reported on his improving physical condition.

Gulag, as a man responsible for fratricidal war in Yugoslavia, and as an oriental despot dressed in the image of an enlightened leader suitable for Western tastes. Finally, (at least in the last years of his life) he remained to many the mastermind of huge deficits, of a ruined economy with high unemployment, and a twenty-two billion dollar foreign debt. The fickleness of reputation, of course, is well known in history:

> Had Hitler succeeded in his plan of conquest, even partially or in particular, undoubtedly he would have been hailed by many as the world's greatest leader.
>
> Had Kruschev not found it advantageous to his career to expose Stalin's crimes (and the Gulag system) he [Stalin] would have been regarded by many as a demi-god ...[8]
>
> A brilliant politician and a coward, a proletarian who enjoyed royal splendor, a critic of the Stalin cult and a cult on his own: Tito was a phenomenon stranger than a science-fiction and as paradoxical as the experiment which bears his name[9].

Unlike his contemporaries in other communist countries – like Klement Gottwald of Czechoslovakia and Imre Nagy of Hungary – who were either imposed or deposed through the mercies of the Kremlin, Tito succeeded in leaving a lasting imprint on Yugoslavia as an independent, communist dictator and founder of a communist state. During his reign Yugoslavs became accustomed to using Tito's name synonymously with the concept of communist Yugoslavia, which many perceived as his creation. Consequently, the idea of Titoism as a peculiar form of Yugoslav communist ideology became so powerful that it succeeded in surviving its founder. Stating it more bluntly, as *Der Spiegel* did, "The cult of the living Tito was replaced in 1980 with the cult of the dead Tito"[10].

Tito's rejection of Soviet influence in the years after 1948 was wrongly interpreted in the West as his refusal of Stalinism and acceptance of a somewhat more liberal communism. It must be emphasized that Tito's communism was never meant to question what Lenin created and Stalin later implemented. Tito's opposition to Stalin can in no way be interpreted as his abandonment of communism. Marxist ideology was the only legally accepted body of beliefs in Yugoslavia and Tito and his followers considered themselves as its only real offspring. Edward Kardelj, Tito's "right hand" and the official party ideologist, once stated that "The Yugoslav form of socialism entitles each citizen to real freedom and full democracy and ties it consis-

---

8 Oskar Gruenwald, *The Yugoslav Search for Man* (South Hadley: J. F. Bergin Publishers, Inc., 1983), p. 269.

9 Gruenwald; Ibid, p. 269-270.

10 *Der Spiegel*; "Vom Titokult zum Totenkult," May 12, 1980.

tantly with Marxism and Leninism"[11]. Titoist Yugoslavia should not be considered as some sort of "enfant terrible" of the Third Communist International because of its apparently warm approach to the West and rather cool attitude toward the Soviet Union. During its existence Yugoslavia never attempted to sway into the orbit of the West, nor did it reform its Marxist ideology in spite of the Western assumption that reciprocity would suffice to readjust Yugoslavia to Western standards.

Communist countries around the world often disputed the nature of the "scientific" implementation of Marxism. Each assumed to be the only true repository of Marxism and they rarely tolerated the accusation of being "revisionists" or having betrayed the "Marxist cause". Tito's Yugoslavia was the first country to embrace communism outside the Soviet Union, but it was also the first to walk out of the Cominform[12]. Driven by Soviet pressures and lured by Western credits, Titoists abandoned some of the more visible signs of doctrinaire communism and led Yugoslavia toward adopting some "bourgeois" characteristics which were hardly compatible with the ideas upon which the regime had been founded. Despite these cosmetic changes, Tito never attempted to alter the totalitarian structure of Yugoslavia of which the Marxist doctrine and communist practices remained the same as in the Soviet Union. Indeed, in order to demonstrate his firm communist beliefs, Tito often resorted to the same repressive measures against his internal opponents that he had learned under Stalin while in Moscow. Ironically, Tito can also be described as a dissident leader within the international communist movement, while at the same time he never tolerated the presence of dissidence on Yugoslav soil.

It must be conceded that Titoist Yugoslavia, despite the closed character of its society, was not entirely leak-proof against influences seeping in from the West and the East. Sometimes, these influences affected the nature of Titoism and the role of dissidence, as well as modifying Yugoslavia's political development. Titoist Yugoslavia was successful in keeping itself away from Soviet and American tutelage, notwithstanding the fact that it borrowed its ideology from the East and its foreign aid from the West. Yugoslavia's non-aligned status was Tito's masterful achievement which preserved his legacy and made him a prestigious leader in the international

---

11 Edvard Kardelj, *Sabrana dela* (Beograd: Prosveta, 1980), p. 18.

12 Name given to the Communist Information Bureau, an agency of international communism founded under the auspicies of the Soviet Union in 1947. "The most vehement supporters of the Cominform were the Yugoslav communists." Quoted from the *Encyclopedia Britannica*, Micropaedia, 15th ed. (Chicago: Encyclopaedia Britannica, Inc., 1983), p. 35.

community. Alternatively, the independence of Yugoslavia may also have had its shortcomings. In difficult times, Yugoslavia found itself short of allies, forced to rely on its own domestic resources to protect its stability. If one of the superpowers had decided to destabilize Yugoslavia, it remains questionable whether the other superpower would have been willing to save Yugoslavia's Titoism.

Totalitarianism is a term applied to modern autocratic states which – by means of a monolithic political party or dictator, repressive methods, and the total control of information – instill in its citizens a sacrosanct ideology to which everybody must conform. All totalitarian states are in opposition to democratic principles; a plurality and diversity of ideas is not tolerated and is systematically eradicated. According to Hannah Arendt,

> Loneliness, the common ground for terror, is the essence of totalitarian government; it prepares its executioners and its victims, and is closely connected with uprootedness and superfluousness. Whereas tyrannies and despotisms, based on isolation, generally leave the productive capacity of the man intact, the totalitarian state, by means of suspicion and fear, aim at the systematic destruction of man's creativity[13].

The totalitarian state is a 20th century phenomenon. There are still many misunderstandings and different interpretations of totalitarianism. Some authors use the word interchangeably with authoritarianism. The concept of totalitarianism is almost always subject to a political point of view. A "leftist" will hardly ever call the Soviet Union a totalitarian state; at worst, it is an authoritarian state. In contrast, Chile and the Philippines were invariably depicted as totalitarian. A few thinkers of the Frankfurt School (Herbert Marcuse, Theordor Adorno, Max Horkheimer, and others) argued that the United States was no less totalitarian than the Soviet Union. They contend that the total control of American citizens is not being carried out by mass killings or Gulags, but rather through the systematic "soft" conditioning of the media; as Ernst Bloch, another "leftist" thinker, phrases it, "through a non-stop light show." In recent years the French New Right – which has nothing to do with the American New Right, save its virulent anti-communism – has also adopted a view that the *homo economicus* of Western democracies has become pacified and alienated as a result of the total "mediasation" of his public and private life[14].

---

13 Hannah Arendt, *The Origins of Totalitarianism* (New York: Harcourt Brace, Inc., 1955), p. 475.

14 See the excellent *Le Système à tuer les peuples* by Guillaume Faye (Paris: Edition Copernic, 1981).

One may question the extent to which Western democracies contain elements of totalitarianism, but it is beyond the scope of this thesis to analyze totalitarianism in countries other than Yugoslavia. The above discussion is included here only as an example of how difficult it is to arrive at a consensus concerning the concept of totalitarianism among European intellectuals. The best definition of totalitarianism, in the author's view, has been given by Michael Curtis:

> These other types of regimes [dictatorships, despotisms, autocratic regimes, tyrannies] leave a whole area of life untouched by official control. The totalitarian system embodies not only strong and arbitrary power, it also insists on conformity, mass mobilization, subjugation, suspicion and atomization in society[15].

Even if repression exists in authoritarian states, such states are not inherently opposed to the cultural sphere of life. This is not the case for the communist totalitarian state, where culture must conform to Marxist standards. For the communist, culture is for the bourgeois and must, consequently, be erased from the minds of people as a form of reactionary delinquency. Creativity, itself, is necessarily an act of dissidence in the communist state.

There were several structural characteristics of Yugoslav totalitarianism:

1. Communist party control of the state and its executive organs.
2. Communist party control of the economy ("self-management").
3. Communist party control of Yugoslav social and cultural life.
4. The Communist party as a synonym of state control and repository of Titoism.

Yugoslavs were generally led to believe that their state was a democracy, and absolutely no references was ever made to its totalitarian structure. After forty years the state instilled in the minds of Yugoslavs that Titoist communism remains the only historical answer to their social and private problems. Past and present menaces which lingered in Yugoslav society were constantly supplemented by promises of a better future. In some respects, it can be said that Yugoslavia created a new man, *homo duplex*, or in the words of Alexander Zinoviev, *homo sovieticus*[16].

This *homo duplex* from Yugoslavia was typified, on the one hand, by persistent hope for a future earthly paradise which will place him ahead of his Western neighbors, and on the other hand, by a profound feeling of apa-

---

15 Michael Curtis, *Totalitarianism* (New Brunswick: Transaction Books, 1980), p. 3.

16 A name of the book carries the same title: *Homo Sovieticus* by Alexander Zinoviev (Lausanne: Diogenes Verlag, 1983).

thy which often became transformed into political fatalism and a refusal to assume responsibility for one's own destiny. Since his private interests must be submitted to the omnipotent interests of the state system, there is no motive-power left to use his productive capacity in order to enhance his own life. Personal assets such as intelligence, creativity and wit are actually supressed because they are antithetical to the state's idea of forced "equalitarianism"[17]. No wonder that measuring human intelligence with IQ tests was always considered in Yugoslavia as a bourgeois relic – as seen that way by many in the West as well! – incompatible with political priorities. A person sticking out in the crowd, be he a delinquent or a genius, causes embarassment in this Procrustean system and must be set aside. Totalitarianism was well entrenched in Yugoslavia. It was internalized by the citizenry, creating self-coercion and self-suspicion; overt repression was generally no longer necessary[18]. Suspicion, false rumors, exaggerated fear of the secret police ("Udbophobia") – all these paralyzed the entire population and made social contacts increasingly painful, not to mention looking at one's self in the mirror[19].

Relationship Between Yugoslav Dissidence and Titoism

Yugoslav dissidents lacked a common political platform which might have sustained them in their fight against Titoist Yugoslavia and legitimized in the eyes of Western observers. Often, Yugoslav dissidents dissented against each other, crippling their own credibility and fostering the credibility of the Titoists. Ironically, some Yugoslav dissidents, instead of weakening the Titoists, actually weakened their own positions. The Yugoslav communist authorities exploited this weakness of the nationalist dissidents by setting one group against the other; thus, neutralizing each group one by one[20].

Occasionally, the authorities even resorted to the artificial creation of domestic dissidence in order to invigorate their own failing image. Absurd cases of "state enemies" would be widely reported by the state-controlled

---

17 The pathology of communism, the distorted and aberrant behavior of those who suffer under it, has been successfully described by Alexander Zinoviev, *The Reality of Communism* (New York: Schocken Books, 1984) and Louis Rougier, *La Mystique démocratique* (Paris: Edition Albatros, 1983).

18 See Zinoviev, *The Reality of Communism*, "The Irreversibility of Social Evolution," p. 259.

19 The UDBA (Uprava Drzavne Bezbednosti) was the name of the Yugoslav secret police.

20 Croatian emigrants published over 40 different journals and periodicals in the West, each of which typically attacked some other one.

press, the purpose of which was to divert public opinion away from real problems and onto ficticious ones[21].

One may raise the question of whether Titoism, as such, could have been fully successful without the unwitting support of its local dissidents. In his essay on communism and the psychology of revolutionaries, Berdyayev observes that for a communist, the world must be clearly divided between good and evil, "between the kingdoms of Ormuzd and Ahriman with no shading in between"[22]. In Yugoslavia, Titoists considered themselves the good guys and depicted dissidents as the bad guys. And yet, at the same time, the Titoists needed dissidents as an historical necessity, an antithesis which helps justify and legitimize the communists' maintenance of power. (Had the dissidents disappeared altogether, Titoists would almost certainly have disappeared along with them.)

It was often said in Yugoslavia that dissidents spoke aloud what most Yugoslavs thought silently. Many Yugoslavs were potential dissidents, but only a few dared publicly voice their critical opinions about Titoism. The major reason which kept them from open criticism was fear of repression and police reprisals against their families. Titoism proved to be a quasi-irreversible ideology, and the longer it endured, the less justification the dissidents could find to successfully question it:

> A long established system of government will always finally seem acceptable to the people governed. Habit masks its inconveniences, which appear only when men begin to think[23].

Yugoslav "inconveniences" were evident to all Yugoslavs, not only to the dissidents who unmasked them. Fighting against a system which had been static and irrevocable for more than forty years amounted to political suicide. The overwhelming fear that they might have been arrested at any moment, interrogated, tortured or even killed – and all within the certitude of knowing that the Western world will never find out about it – increased the potential dissidents' apathy and led them toward political opportunism.

Western countries occasionally criticized the human rights record of Titoist Yugoslavia although, the results of such criticism were rejected by the authorities as "undemocratic meddling into Yugoslavia's internal affairs." The recent history of Europe demonstrates that totalitarian systems

---

21 Communist daily newspapers in Yugoslavia (such as *Borba, Vjesnik* or *Politika*) had special columns which discussed "state enemies".

22 Berdyayev; ibid., p. 184.

23 Gustav Le Bon, *La Révolution française et la psychologie des révolutions* (Paris: Gallimard, 1936), p. 138.

permit the worst transgressions over human rights, so long as they are supported by ideology. In the case of Yugoslavia, this ideology was Titoism, which hid its repression or justified it by means of Marxist dialectics. Repression in Yugoslav daily life could be countered either by overt opportunism or, in the case of the dissident, a covert low profile.

For many Yugoslavs, dissidents were like a scourge starting fires or causing epidemics of plague. The population, seized by political apathy, often considered dissidents as "troublemakers" who were likely to incite the authorities to more indiscriminate repression. Dissidents were, therefore, often avoided, even by closest family members. For the average Yugoslav, dissidents were a "taboo theme", which could be discussed only in complete privacy and then only with a great deal of reluctance[24].

Summary of Chapter I

The purpose of the Chapter I has been to acquaint the reader with Yugoslav communism and Yugoslav dissidence. A brief historical survey of the South-Slav nations was given in order to better explain the ethnic complexity of politics and dissidence in Yugoslavia.

The section on Titoism and totalitarianism attempted to demonstrate that, despite minor differences, Yugoslav communism was very similar to Soviet communism. Yugoslav communism, known as Titoism, followed the same pattern of terror, persecution and fear.

Titoism originated during World War II, a war that was particularly devastating in Yugoslavia. During this war, five different armies and national factions were fighting each other in occupied Yugoslavia.

World War II gave momentum to the civil war and swept Yugoslavia into chaos. It was during this chaos that Tito managed to lay the foundations of his future communist state. On his road to power in Yugoslavia, Tito succeeded in silencing the non-communist factions and, by 1945, fully consolidated his firm grip on the Yugoslav communist movement.

---

24 See a very instructive article by Nora Beloff in *The Times* (London), November 11, 1984.

Chapter II: The Rise of Titoism and Yugoslav Dissidents: 1941-1945

Introduction

This chapter has several objectives. First, it discusses the events which brought about the disintegration of the old Yugoslav monarchy and the subsequent German invasion of Yugoslavia. Second, it traces the causes and consequences of the civil war in Yugoslavia and the atrocities committed by the various warring factions. The third part of this chapter provides some explanation of how and why the Titoists, and not some other faction, ascended to power in Yugoslavia.

It will be seen that Tito owes his victory not to the numerical strength of his partisans, but primarily to favorable external circumstances. Tito's armed resistance against the occupants began in the first days of the German invasion of the Soviet Union and continued until the end of the war. When the Allies won the war, Tito was rewarded for his relentless fight against fascism both by the Soviets and the Western powers. Consequently, Tito's ascendency to power in Yugoslavia was facilitated by the Soviets and Americans: It was an Allied gift to the man who seemingly fought simultaneously for communist ideals as well as the ideals of Western democracy.

Internal Struggles Between National Factions

The outbreak of World War II in Europe caught Yugoslavia in the midst of a feud between Serbs and Croats and politically unprepared for resistance to the rising tide of fascism. Except for the Serbs, who were in the majority, the other nations of Yugoslavia lacked the Yugoslav sentiment and showed reluctance to defend a monarchy which they perceived as a symbol of national opression. Croats were opposed to the idea of preserving the state of Yugoslavia and awaited the first opportunity to establish their own independent state. With the German invasion of 1941, the artificial unity and consensus of Yugoslavia's diverse nations disappeared and left the country torn by its various, hostile factions. Separatism was at the heart of the ensuing disintegration and not, as some historians assume, Germany's direct aggression[1].

It it often forgotten that Hitler's initial plan for the Balkans was to keep Yugoslavia out of the war in order to secure the German passage to Greece and the Mediterranean Basin. Due to Hitler's pressure, the Yugoslav Monarchy signed the tripartite pact with Germany, Italy, and Japan on March 25, 1941 and thus became part of the German sphere of influence, while maintaining independence in domestic affairs. In return, Germany offered to guarantee the inviolability of Yugoslav territory, protecting it against any invader, particularly Italy. Moreover, Berlin guaranteed that neither German or Italian soldiers (not even convoys of the wounded) nor transports of arms would enter Yugoslav territory, and that Yugoslavia would never be asked to enter the war against any country[2].

Whether Hitler's proposal was sincere is questionable, but considering Hitler's plans for the Soviet Union, it is quite likely that he preferred a neutral and pacified Yugoslavia to an independent Croatia waging war against Serbs and communists and necessitating firm German support. Hitler could not forsee that Croatian dissidents, at home and abroad, did not care vey much about Yugoslavia's political orientation as long as it remained Yugoslavia. He also did not fully comprehend the traditional animosity of Serbs against Germans nor Serbia's historic ties with France and England.

On March 27, 1941, only two days after Yugoslavia's accession to the pact, a handful of Yugoslav military officers of Serbian origin, dissatisfied with the tripartate pact and afraid of rising Croatian separatism, staged a coup d'etat[3]. They overthrew the king and openly rebuked Yugoslavia's adherence to the Axis powers. Eight days later troops from Germany, Bulgaria, Hungary and Italy invaded Yugoslavia and helped the radical Croatian elements, known as the "Ustashi", proclaim an independent Croatia and wiped other parts of former Yugoslavia off the map.

Hitler's consent to the proclamation of an independent Croatia was not motivated by his sensitivity to historical Croatian national aspirations; rather, it was the move of a man who, by the logic of "realpolitik", looked for a solid stronghold in the exasperating and ethnically-torn Balkans.

---

1 That Germany was responsible for the disintegration of Yugoslavia was the view held by all Yugoslav historians, who seldom analyzed the causes of the disintegration. See Vladimir Dedijer and Milorad Ekmecic, *History of Yugoslavia* (New York: MacGraw-Hill, Inc., 1974).

2 Ilija Jukic, *The Fall of Yugoslavia* (New York: Harcourt Brace Jovanovich, 1974), pp. 54, 59.

3 There are unproved allegations that the Serbian officers were incited by the British to stage a coup d'etat and abrogate the Pact with Germany.

Given the fact that Hitler had already postponed his campaign against the Soviets because of Yugoslavia, the idea of restoring the old monarchy as an alternative to the creation of Croatia may have appeared to him as a waste of precious time[4].

Tito's Role

Before the outbreak of World War II Tito was an obscure leader of about 12,000 Yugoslav communists who had very little popular support among the general population of Yugoslavia. Official Yugoslav historians, who were otherwise very epic in their description of Tito's heroic role during the guerilla war against the Germans, rarely spoke about his pre-war activities. Before he became a prominent partisan leader, Tito lived alternately in Yugoslavia and the Soviet Union and he closely followed the directives issued by Stalin. He was also one of the rare communist leaders who survived the Stalinist purges of the 1930's[5]. Some Yugoslav dissidents accused Tito of collaboration with Stalin and criticized the methods he used to get rid of his cumbersome comrades and assure his ascendency in the Yugoslav Communist Party.

In the first days following the German invasion, Tito and his followers did not automatically begin armed resistance. Contrary to his official biographers, who credit Tito as the first to conduct open guerilla warfare against occupying German troops, Tito first waited for instructions from Moscow and began armed resistance in Yugoslavia only after the Nazi invasion of the Soviet Union had begun. The non-agression pact which Germany signed with the Soviet Union in 1939 was a sacrosanct document for all European communist leaders, including Tito, and they abided by it as long as the integrity of the Soviet Union was not violated. Indeed, it can be argued that Tito's communists passively collaborated with the Nazis from April to June of 1941, from the time Germany invaded Yugoslavia to the time Germany began invading the Soviet Union. For Tito, the German invasion of the Soviet Union alone marked the beginning of his unconditional and irreversible

---

4 Yugoslav historians argued that Hitler's invasion of the Soviet Union had failed because of his campaign in Yugoslavia and the consequent delay in the invasion of the Soviet Union. See Vladimir Dedijer, *Tito* (New York: Simon and Schuster, 1953). The book is a masterful piece of communist hagiography.

5 The principal leaders of the Yugoslav Communist Party before the war, Gorkic and Copic, were executed in the Soviet Union in 1939 by the NKVD. Both are known to have been in strong disagreement with Tito. According to rough estimates, several hundred Yugoslav communist leaders perished in the Stalin purges before World War II.

fight against Germany and German-sponsored Croatia. Tito's armed struggle also represented a further step toward establishing a Soviet Yugoslavia and eliminating the vestiges of the old constitutional monarchy.

In order to succeed in his anti-fascist and anti-monarchical endeavors, Tito needed the support of all the nations and ethnic groups of Yugoslavia; his communists could not do it alone. Creating a common revolutionary zeal in the heterogeneous population of Yugoslavia remained Tito's most daring task; it was accomplished through exploiting the weaknesses of one nation, setting it against the other, and molding the discontented elements into one cohesive communist movement. Tito's principal enemies were the occupying Germans and the radical Croatian nationalists who, weeks after the proclamation of the state of Croatia, raised a fully operational army. Tito's enemies also included the anti-communist Serbs, the remnants of the royal forces who were violently opposed to the disintegration of Yugoslavia, the establishment of a separate Croatia, as well as the rise of Tito to the status of the sole anti-fascist leader in Yugoslavia.

Each faction had its inherent shortcomings and common hatred of its rival. The Croatian Ustashi – due to their indiscriminate persecution of the Serbian minorities in Croatia, Bosnia and Hercegovina – soon lost their prestige among those Croats who initially sympathized with their cause. The Ustashi persecution of Serbs rose to such proportions that it soon drove many Serbs into the ranks of Titoist partisans and created a lingering mistrust between these two nations. Even moderate and democratically-minded Croats, who became disturbed by the pogrom against the Serbs, began joining Tito's partisans. Their motives were not ideological; rather, to them Titoism was a matter of survival. Many of them nourished the hope that after the war Tito, being a Croat himself, would respect the autonomy of Croatia and establish a democracy in which Serbs would no longer have the upper hand.

The Serbian royalist forces, known as the Chetniks, did not have much success against the Germans either. Their influence was confined to Serbia proper and, despite their pro-Yugoslav rhetoric and occasional harrassment of German troops stationed in Serbia, they could not mobilize a single Croat. The Chetniks were the first faction to begin armed resistance against occupying forces, but during the following years their role became increasingly passive and finally adopted a "wait and see" tactic. Furthermore, crimes committed by the Chetniks against the Croatian Moslems and Albanian separatists, as well as their habit of ritually killing captives, eroded the Chetnik image among the Western Allies. Indeed, the only group to benefit from this fratricidal chaos was Tito's partisans, the only supra-national force which successfully opposed the Chetniks, the Germans and the fascist-sponsored Ustashi. The Titoists never favored one nation more than another during the war.

The War Within the War

By 1942, World War II was well under way and the continuous presence of Germans and Italians only exacerbated the prevailing civil war among different Yugoslav factions. This dismal situation in Yugoslavia, this war within a war with its horrifying factional violence, found expression in a book written by Milovan Djilas, one of the most prominent Serbian communist partisans, a later Yugoslav hero and a future dissident,

> ... the human devastation inside [the town of Foca] was immeasurable and inconceivable. In the spring of 1941 the Ustashi – among them a good number of Moslem toughs – had killed many Serbs. Then the Chetniks occupied the little town and proceeded to slaughter the Moslems. Four hundred Serbs and three thousand Moslems were reported killed in the region of Foca[6].

The civil war in Yugoslavia, combined with frequent reprisals by the Germans against Titoist partisans, took a toll of more than one million lives during the span of four years. Those who suffered most were defenseless civilians from all ethnic groups who were dragged involuntarily into the senseless carnage; they began seeing Tito's multi-ethnic partisans forces as the only form of redemption. It should be explained that the majority of Yugoslavs had very vague notions of the meanings of fascism or Tito's communism. In a country where, before the war, eighty percent of the population were peasants, tribal feelings of the most rudimentary survivalism prevailed over all manner of political ideologies.

It cannot be argued that Chetniks and Ustashi were destined to commit their civil-war crimes. The causes are more complex and can be attributed to a Yugoslav monarchy which had not attempted to solve the intra-national frictions before the war by developing a solid framework for the democratic coexistance of Yugoslavia's respective nations. Additionally, one must look to the failures of the Treaties of Versailles, Trianon, and Saint Germain, which resulted in the creation of the artificial state of Yugoslavia under Serbian supervision, as a major cause of sharpened intra-ethnic conflict in Yugoslavia and subsequent civil war. Also, none of the factions can be more or less justified or condemned for their respective violence. Tito's partisans

6 Milovan Djilas, *Wartime* (New York: Harcourt Brace Jovanovich, 1977), p. 139.

were just as ferocious as the other factions; none of the factions took prisoners and the laws of land warfare were hardly ever respected in this remote part of the rugged Balkan mountains:

> No prisoners were taken; they were just shot down by the same peasants who had also attacked our [partisan] field hospitals. Some seven thousand were killed around four hundred escaped. No one liked to speak of this particular experience – not even those who made a show of their revolutionary spirit ...[7].

Lack of Consensus Among Exiled Yugoslav Representatives

On the day of the Axis invasion of Yugoslavia, Yugoslav King Petar Karadjordjevic and his closest advisors fled the country and established headquarters in Washington and London under the auspicies of the Allied forces. The exiled Yugoslav government in its new environment reflected precisely the same ethnic divergencies as seen on the wider scale in pre-war Yugoslavia. With the exception of a few Croatians and Slovenians, ninety percent of the politicians were Serbs, including the King, himself. Soon, the familiar factional bickering which had plagued the monarchy before the war began anew and started poisoning the precarious relationships among the respective Yugoslav politicians.

Even though all the Yugoslav diplomats were antifascists and against the Nazi dismemberment of Yugoslavia, they were unable to reach any unanimous agreements on how the fight against the occupying troops should be conducted. Serbian politicians overemphasized the role of the Chetniks as the only truly pro-western Yugoslav movement; although, as noted above, the Chetniks remained Serbian-oriented to the end of the war. Serbian politicians also minimized Chetnik crimes against the Croats, while exaggerating the crimes committed by the Ustashi against the Serbian population in Croatia. Likewise, Croatian representatives in the exiled government disliked the Allies excessively portraying Croatia as an artificial, fascist state engaged in murderous practices and were disturbed by the glorification of the Chetnik guerilla[8]. This atmosphere of mutual distrust between Serbian and Croatian politicians in exile became so intense that, in the long run, it impeded any solution in favor of Yugoslavia and effective resistance against the Axis powers.

---

7 Djilas, Ibid., p. 448.

8 *London Times*, September 29, 1943.

Juraj Krnjevich and Ivan Subasich, two Croatian politicians in the exiled goverment, represented the remnants of the Croatian Peasant Party which had been at odds with the monarchy ever since the assassination of its leader, Stjepan Radic, in 1928[9]. The Croatian Peasant Party never condoned the creation of a fascist-sponsored Croatia; although, it was equally opposed to Serbian supremacy in Yugoslavia. The Croatian Peasant Party envisioned the future of Croatia as a completely autonomous state, yet within a Yugoslav confederation. Such views about autonomy were hardly tolerated by the Serbian representatives, who saw in them the prelude to a separate Croatia and a challenge to Serbian efforts to bring about a unitary Yugoslavia. The atmosphere which reigned in the Allied capitals is best understood through the words of Serbian Ambassador Constantin Fotich: "Dr. Krnjevich seemed more interested in bringing independence to Croatia than in the reestablishment of Yugoslavia as a state"[10]. From such incriminations it can be concluded that the situation among Yugoslavs abroad was no better than among Yugoslavs at home, with the exception that those abroad did not shoot at one another. It will be seen in Chapter IV that to some extent the Yugoslav presence abroad was of equal importance to the fratricidal war in Yugoslavia.

Military developments in Yugoslavia soon brought an end to the constant bickering among exiled Yugoslavs. With help from the Allies, Tito's slow, but persistant success over all the Yugoslav national factions left the exiled politicians disillusioned over the possible restoration of the monarchy. The mutual accusations and overt hatred between Serbs and Croats, plus the inability of the government in exile to reach any agreement concerning the future of Yugoslavia, left a very negative impression on their Allied hosts:

> Even the relations between American descendants of these two people worsened ... so that the American government seriously worried that it might endanger domestic peace in the USA[11].

Under such circumstances, Allied forces were unable to gain an accurate picture of what was really going on in Yugoslavia. The information they *did receive* was often contradictory. Given the fact that at the same time Tito's partisans were gaining significant military results, the Allies decided to

---

9 Stjepan Radic, founder of the Croatian Peasant Party and a father of modern democratic Croatia, was assassinated in the Yugoslav Assembly in Belgrade in 1928 during a debate with some Serbian politicians. His death gave momentum to the radical Ustashi movement led by Dr. Ante Pavelic.

10 Constantin Fotich, *The War We Lost* (New York: Viking Press, 1948), p. 129.

11 Fotich, Ibid., p. 132.

switch camps and began supporting Tito's forces. At the 1943 summit meeting in Teheran, Churchill, Roosevelt, and Stalin agreed to provide Tito's forces with all necessary help. The immediate results of this Allied decision were four-fold:

1. Internationally, it dealt a serious blow to Germany and forced Hitler to move more troops to the Balkans.

2. It demoralized the anti-communist, pro-western Chetniks and discredited the Croatian Ustashi state.

3. It projected Tito into the limelight of international politics and reassured him of Allied help in becoming a future leader.

4. It set the stage for the Yalta agreement and helped expand communism in Eastern Europe.

Allied Recognition of Tito and the End of the War

In early 1945, despite the approaching Allied victory and the help he was receiving, Tito was still a long way from seizing power over the whole of Yugoslavia. Other Eastern European nations – Poland, Czechoslovakia, Hungary, Romania and Bulgaria – were already under the firm control of the Red Army. Although the war was over for many, it was not over for Tito who still had not managed to clear Serbia of the Chetnik presence, let alone deal a serious blow to Croatia. Various anti-communist and pro-German militias continued to fight successfully against Tito's partisans. For many, this was only a civil war and they largely ignored the significance of the major world events, conferences and agreements which would so dramatically affect their future. Contrary to Titoist officials, the latter claiming that the entire population was behind them by the end of 1944, the civil war in Yugoslavia probably would have lasted much longer had the Yalta agreement and the armistice not been signed in February and May of 1945, respectively[12].

Tito's victory came quickly and can be attributed more to the Allied victory in general than to Tito's military successes in particular. After the war, the role of Tito's partisans was considerably magnified, as if they had been destined to win, regardless of other circumstances which might have been less favorable. It should be noted that by the end of 1944 the Soviet Army was solidly entrenched all around Yugoslavia, and their mere presence could reasonably have assured Tito of his communist victory. The truth

---

[12] The Yalta agreement was signed by Stalin, Roosevelt and Churchill on February 11, 1945.

is, however, that the Red Army only played a slight role in the military operations of Yugoslavia; for example, the Red Army coming from Romania helped in the partisan "liberation" of Belgrade. From 1945 to 1948, when Tito broke with Stalin, the role of the Red Army was glorified, only to be minimized in the following years. In the last month of the war, Tito probably knew that Yugoslavia was a special case among Eastern European states, being more a part of the Western Allied sphere of influence; hence, his apprehension in 1944 that he might perish along with his partisans in case the Allied forces reached some decision unfavorable to his movement.

It is difficult to say why the Soviets did not "liberate" Yugoslavia in late 1944 during their campaign in Romania. What separated the Red Army from Ustashi-run Croatia and Serbian Chetniks was nothing more than the Panonian Plain[13]. One can even argue that the Soviets were ideologically obliged to do that, given the fact that their man, Tito, was fighting an unnecessarily prolonged war. There are various hypothesis which try to account for Soviet reluctance to help Tito's partisans, allowing them to fight virtually alone until the last minute:

1. Over half a million German troops were still deployed in the Balkans, representing a serious threat to the Soviet advance.

2. The Soviets were heavily involved in the processes of denazification and pacification of the newly "liberated" Hungary, Romania and Bulgaria. Having suffered heavy losses during their campaign, no resources were available for a further advance toward Yugoslavia.

3. The Soviets were always reluctant to accept Yugoslavia as a state because they considered it a creation of Versailles; they never fully considered it a legitimate political entity, be it communist or anti-communist. Yugoslavia's disintegration in April, 1941, was welcomed by the Soviets who were tied by the German-Soviet Pact until June of this year. With the German invasion of Yugoslavia, the Soviets ousted the Yugoslav ambassador and helped justify for two months the creation of fascist-sponsored Croatia.

These ideas help explain why Tito broke away from Stalin in 1948, and why the Titoist policy toward the Soviet Union had always been based on suspicion and caution. As argued above, Tito's revolution was motivated and facilitated more by prevailing national conflicts and less by Marxist principles. For Tito, partisan guerilla warfare meant cementing forever Yugoslav unity under the popular slogan, "brotherhood and unity". For the Soviets, perhaps, it was precisely the other way around: Securing first the communist victory, regardless of whether the region was a single state or several. Nev-

---

13 The Pannonian Plain borders Yugoslavia on the north and east and stretches out to Hungary.

ertheless, until 1948 Yugoslav historians wrote about the Titoist revolution as coordinated and carried out together with the Soviets. After 1949, scarcely any reference to Soviet involvement was made, and for all the war achievements in Yugoslavia, only Tito and his partisans were credited.

In 1944, under Allied pressure, Tito conceded to form a provisional coalition government including some exiled politicians of the old Yugoslav regime. The King appointed Dr. Subasich as his plenipotentiary representative. For Tito, this was an uneasy choice; after four years of bitter guerilla warfare he had to give in to British pressure and welcome a man who was antagonistic to his revolutionary aspirations. On the other hand, if Tito had rejected the nomination of Subasich, who was backed by the Yugoslav king and the Allies, it would have been equivalent to his political suicide. Tito, therefore, had to devise a method of appeasing the West while at the same time securing his future, i.e. independent communist leadership in Yugoslavia. In those decisive months, Tito was still a long way from final victory; in Serbia, he could count on few sympathizers and Croatia was still controlled by Ustashi units and the retreating German army.

Even if the war had come to an abrupt end, bringing the defeat of Nazism, this would still have meant the continuation of Tito's struggle against rival factions. Besides, neither the British nor the Soviets could guarantee Tito that he would emerge some day as the only legitimate leader of Yugoslavia. Historians have demonstrated that it is much easier to rationalize achievements in the past than to project them with the same certainty into the future. For Titoists, after the war, everything was officially interpreted according to Marxist dialectical logic, according to which victory was self-explanatory and imminent[14].

To satisfy the West and gain more time, Tito reluctantly accepted Subasich in his provisional government, but shortly thereafter forced Subasich into premature retirement. Thus, Subasich was the first to suffer the tragedy which would some months later be the common fate of his friends and contemporaries: Benes, King Michael, Ferenc Nagy and all other Eastern European democratic politicians who nourished excessive hopes of Western support[15].

---

14 See Dedijer, *Tito*. This book excells in the glorification of Titoist deeds, leading the reader to believe that the Titoists were the only faction in war-torn Yugoslavia.

15 Eduard Benes, one of the founders of modern Czechoslovakia, was forced to cooperate with the communists and died a broken man in 1947. King Michael, the Romanian ruler who managed to sever ties with Germany in 1944 and appointed the communist government of Romania, was forced to abdicate in 1947. Ferencz Nagy, the Hungarian Premier in 1945-46 was threatened by communists and escaped to Austria, and then to USA in 1947. See *Der Spiegel*, "So weit die Armeen kommen," September 10, 1984.

The belief that the West, especially the USA, would in due time come to their aid was naively shared by all Yugoslav factions. The Ustashi understood the end of the war and the signature of the Yalta agreement as something negotiable between the great powers, but nobody dared to envision a situation where the German departure would entail necessarily the departure of the Ustashi. In the last months of the war several Ustashi ministers tried unsuccessfully to sever ties with Germany and attempted to establish relations with the Allies[16]. Somehow, during the last months of the war, everybody in Croatia seemed to have discovered democratic virtues, and references to the Ustashi ties with the Germans and pogroms of the Serbs were forgotten. Up until the last moments, the Ustashi could not fully understand that the state of Croatia, established under the auspicies of Germany, would not readily be accepted by the Allies.

Chetniks held similar illusions. The fact that they had been assigned British military observers until late 1944 led them to firmly believe that the West would know how to appreciate their anti-communist and pro-Yugoslav plight. Chetniks interpreted the endless conferences and agreements between the British, Americans and Soviets as the Allied bolstering of the old regime and encouraging signs for the restoration of royal Yugoslavia. Tito did not harbor such illusions nor did he wait for miracles; although, the miracle for him finally came at Yalta.

In the meantime, Stalin agreed that America and England should share evenly in the influence on Yugoslavia. Stalin and Tito also agreed that a new government be formed in Yugoslavia on the basis of agreements between Tito and Subasich, who several months earlier had visited the Soviet Union. On April 11, 1945 (one month before Croatia was taken by the Titoists) Subasich, Tito and Molotov signed a treaty of friendship. Tito solemnly promised a plebiscite whereby Yugoslavs, in a liberated state, could freely proclaim their political sympathies. This plebiscite was never held, and in November of 1945, six months after the communist take over, a new constitution was adopted, a virtual replica of the Soviet constitution. Thus, Yugoslavia openly became a communist state.

16 Ustashi Ministers, Mladen Lorkovic and Ante Vokic, attempted a coup d'etat against Croatian leader Pavelic in the hope of gaining recognition for Croatia from the Allies. Presumably, they were executed by Pavelic several days before the Croatian army retreated toward Austria. See Jukic, *The Fall of Yugoslavia*.

Appraisal of the War Years in Yugoslavia

The appraisal of World War II and the civil war in Yugoslavia depends upon the standards of judgement employed and upon the person who passes such a judgement. If one takes into consideration the complexity of pre-war Yugoslavia, its unsolved national question and the underlying Serbian supremacy, then it can be argued that the ensuing carnage was a predictable outcome. Historians often dispute among themselves the real causes of the Yugoslav catastrophy and they rarely ever agree on any major issue concerning Yugoslavia's factional fights or Tito's rise to power. Considering the multitude of books on the Yugoslav civil war, and given the divergent opinions of different authors, it remains as difficult today as it was in the years following the war to establish the real causes of the Yugoslav disintegration and the degree of responsibility of each faction. Having in mind that forty years is not enough time to properly assess this tragic period of European history, the researcher is compelled to look for pertinent information from first hand sources which, admittedly, are sometimes of very dubious character and filled with subjective interpretations.

It has already been explained how Titoists interpret the war years and the rise of communism in Yugoslavia. The chaos of the war years, according to Titoists, was an historical necessity which was molded and cemented forever into the two principles of Titoism, "brotherhood and unity", presided over by omnipotent communists. The Titoist part in war crimes is usually obscured in euphemisms, such as "errors", "lack of coordination" or "lack of resources". Unfortunately, those who could really provide more information on this painful period are no longer alive, and Titoists have never been willing to clarify their real history.

Most of the sources published in the West are not accurate, either. Books and accounts written or published by Croatian emigrees in the West usually tend to minimize the extent of Ustashi crimes and often exaggerate the Croatian loss of life after the armistice. Vladimir Macek, a moderate politician and a democrat, but also a Croatian nationalist, writes,

> In the middle of April, 1941 (five days after the proclamation of fascist Croatia), news reached Zagreb of terrible massacres that had blotted out two Croatian villages in Hercegovina. Those responsible for the gruesome deeds were Serbian Chetniks, who had raided the villages two days after the proclamation of the independent State of Croatia. Those who escaped promptly entered Pavelic Ustashi units[17].

---

17 Vladimir Macek, *The Struggle for Freedom* (University Park: The Pennsylvania State University Press, 1948), p. 231.

Macek was under house arrest during the war, having refused to collaborate with the Ustashi; until his death he was equally opposed to radical Ustashi chauvinism and communist Titoism. He continues,

> While the Ustashi pursued their insane policy of Serbian extermination in Croatia, their equally fanatical Serbian counterparts, the Chetniks, undertook to kill off the entire non-Serbian population. The ensuing slaughters were beyond description[18].

It has already been demonstrated how Serbian and pro-Serbian authors describe the same events. Milovan Djilas, a Serbian dissident and a mastermind of Tito's rise to power, only timidly describes the Chetnik crimes while devoting lengthy passages to Ustashi executions. Similar is the view held by some American authors of Serbian descent. For example, in an otherwise pertinent book entitled, *Tito's Promised Land*, Alex Dragnich writes, "The Pavelic Ustashi massacred by the most brutal methods well over a half-million innocent Serbs who lived within the boundaries of Croatia"[19].

Almost identical opinions are held by most Serbs living in the West. How far these unproved allegations can go may best be illustrated by the November 11, 1984 newspaper coverage of the indictment of Dr. Andrija Artukovic in which Ustashi crimes are recounted[20]. Almost all American newspapers, and some European newspapers, presented a story which stated that 850,000 Serbs were killed by the Ustashi. This figure seems very exaggerated since a net decline of 700,000 in the population of Croatia after the war was officially reported, suggesting that it was mostly the Croats who suffered during the war[21]. Even though the exaggerated figures of 850,000 and 700,000 killed Serbs seem cemented in Titoist propaganda, Croatian authors – be they democratic, Ustashi or communist – will never accept it. Even officials of the Titoist government, such as partisan leader and former general Tudjman, dispute these high figures:

---

18 Macek, Ibid., p. 236.

19 Alex Dragnich, *Tito's Promised Land* (New Brunswick: Rutgers University Press, 1954), p. 19.

20 A Minister in the Ustashi Croatian government from 1941 to 1945. After the war he managed to escape to the USA. The Yugoslav communist government and various Jewish groups fought for his extradition to Yugoslavia.

21 Yugoslav communists ascribe this to mass immigration by Croats to Western countries.

Year after year for decades now the assertion has been rammed in the heads of the Yugoslavs that during the Ustashi State, Croatia, in just one camp at Jasenovac there were at least 700,000 people killed and that they were mostly Serbs[22].

In 1965 Tudjman apparently tried to rectify the official figures:

I placed proof before the most responsible people in Croatia that this figure was historically inaccurate, absurd and morally and politically harmful for future Croatio-Serbian relations. [Communists in Croatia] agreed with me, but nothing has been done so far ...[23]

Tudjman continues by citing more accurate figures drafted in 1964, but never published:

Official figures from the Statistical Institute of Croatia drafted in 1964 indicate that on the territory of Croatia there were 185,327 killed of which 59,639 were killed in camps and prisons, 50,000 in direct terror and 68,505 were members of the partisan forces. There are no figures relating the losses of Ustashi and Home Guards[24].

There is no reason to doubt Tudjman's arguments, considering his influential position as a partisan leader and communist general until his imprisonment in 1981. However, while Tudjman related the number of killed Serbs in Croatia proper, he does not include the number of Serbs killed by Ustashi in Bosnia and Hercegovina. Unless a serious effort is made, no one will ever know the exact number of killed Serbs or Croats nor the degree of responsibility of the various warring factions.

Concerning the Croats, they blamed Tito and his zealous partisans for the massacre at Bleiburg, where they claim, over 200,000 Croats were slaughtered during May of 1945. Part of the Croatian grievance is also directed against the British and Allied Field Marshall Alexander, who indiscriminately handed over surrendered Ustashi units together with Croatian civilians to Titoist partisans at the border town of Bleiburg. They were subsequently massacred by Titoist forces. In the collective consciousness of Croats (whether peasants or exiled intellectuals) the town of Bleiburg has almost a mythical significance associated with the largest massacre ever perpetrated on the Croatian people, a massacre they feel offset all Ustashi crimes against the Serbs.

---

22 Franjo Tudjman, *Nationalism in Contemporary Europe* (New York: Columbia University Press, 1981), p. 162.

23 Tudjman, Ibid., p. 163.

24 Tudjman, Ibid., p. 163. (In 1991, after the break-up of communist Yugoslavia, Tudjman became a president of free Croatia.)

Had Tito given amnesty to the Ustashi and prevented the massacre, he would almost certainly have been hampered in his own efforts at building a communist, totalitarian state. Further, the Serbian partisans would probably have never accepted the amnesty of Croatian units. To many Serbs, Tito did not sufficiently carry out the "justice" against the Croats at Bleiburg.

Croatian publications in the West – *Nova Hrvatska, Hrvatska Revija, Danica* and others – usually set the figure of massacred Croats at 250,000. However, it must be mentioned that these publications, despite their democratic attitudes, were sometimes biased and occasionally represented pro-Ustashi sentiments. Oskar Gruenwald, a liberal thinker, claims that the figure given by the Croats is fairly accurate:

> Tito's Gulag archipelago opened with the forced repatriation of some 250,000 Croatian fighters and civilians by the British Military Command in May 1945 ... and the execution of an estimated 80,000 German POW's and the pogrom of German and Hungarian minorities after the war[25].

Gruenwald is not specific enough. The above mentioned figure could imply that the number of killed Croats was even higher if one adds the number of civilians who were possibly killed. Some journalists and authors place the figure of killed Croats at 140,000. Ilija Jukic, a pro-Yugoslav Croat who served as a diplomat in the exiled Yugoslav government, says,

> Tito's people claim that about 120,000 Croats were handed over [by the British]. Croatian sources put the figure much higher, while the figure given by the British and Americans was much lower[26].

In an issue of *Nova Hrvatska* a "Top Secret" facsimile of a British headquarters communique was printed:

> Commander of Allied troops in Austria reports that 200,000 Yugoslav nationals who were serving in German forces have surrendered to him. We would like to turn them over to Marshall Tito immediately ...[27].

This document suggests that the number of killed Yugoslavs (Croats) might have been even higher, considering the civilian population which was retreating along with the Croatian troops, and who were not included in the

---

25 Gruenwald, *The Yugoslav Search for Man*, pp. 272-274.

26 Jukic, *The Fall of Yugoslavia*, p. 283.

27 *Nova Hrvatska*, May 20, 1984 (File N. 151611 B, MACMIS, FX Top Secret, 8th Army, Klagenfurt).

British document. A source from an American Government publication claims that,

> On May 6 Pavelic and his Army fled from Zagreb, while his army and many terrified civilians crossed the border hoping to get protection from the Allies. Their surrender was not accepted by the British, who forced back to Yugoslavia approximately 250,000 Croats ... many of them were immediately executed by the partisans[28].

The above cited passages do not indicate the number of Serbs, Slovenians and ethnic Albanians who were also killed. It might be inferred from the British document that among the "200,000 Yugoslavs" there were a good many Slovenes, Serbs, Montenegrins and other retreating soldiers, such as Hungarians, Bulgarians and even Ukrainians. According to Slovenian sources, over 10,000 Slovenian collaborators (Home Guards) were also executed the same month near the Austro-Yugoslav border. Milovan Djilas, who must have been well aware of these executions, never reports them in his accounts. In most cases, he limits himself to reporting that 7,000 Serbs were killed by the partisans, although these executions took place later in the same year[29]. Since Tito's partisan reprisals continued well into the late 1940's, the above figures must be viewed with considerable tentativeness, for the overall number of executed is probably much higher. Also, no accounts can be found concerning the partisans executions of ethnic Albanians, who were traditionally suspected of separatism and anti-Serbian nationalism. It is very well established that partisans in 1944 carried out several reprisals against ethnic Albanians, yet the number of victims remains unknown.

Summary of Chapter II

In 1939, there were some positive indications that communist and fascist solutions to the Yugoslav national question could have been avoided and the unity of Yugoslavia preserved. Croatian democratic politician Vladimir Macek and a leading Serbian politician, Dragisa Cvetkovic, managed to reach an agreement that would have granted Croatia considerable autonomy and increase pro-Yugoslav sentiments among the diverse peoples. Unfortunately, this agreement was alternatively challenged by radical Croatian nationalists and radical Serbian politicians.

---

28 Richard F. Nyrop, ed., *Yugoslavia: A Country Study* (Washington, D.C.: The American University/Secretary of the Army, 1982), p. 34.

29 Chetnik bands were fighting partisan units unsuccessfully until 1947.

The war swept away the weak foundations of the Serbo-Croatian rapprochement, provoking lasting hatred and mutual incriminations on both sides. During the Yugoslav monarchy the political instability was amplified by the myopic and adventureous Great Serbian policy, which finally had disasterous results for both Croats and Serbs. Further, Croatian Ustashi elements trained in Mussolini's Italy and Horthy's Hungary stubbornly impeded the consensus between moderate Croats and Serbs. In the last analysis, in royal Yugoslavia not a single politician or party existed which could transcend the regional and national lines and appeal to the larger Yugoslav population.

Concerning the communists, thanks to their secrecy and conspiracy, and above all to their supra-national and pro-Yugoslav struggle, the stage was set for their ultimate victory. Several pertinent reasons for the Titoist victory can be stated:

1. Disciplined organization.
2. Clear propaganda.
3. Location of guerilla encampments in the inaccessable mountains of Bosnia and Hercegovina.
4. The backing by the Red Army during the war.
5. Allied recognition of Tito.

During the period of the war Titoists also successfully exploited the surge of radical, pro-fascist elements in Yugoslavia which discredited the latter and pushed the former in a more favorable light. Those Yugoslav politicians and intellectuals who could have acted as a counterweight to Tito's irresistable rise to power were either silenced or too apethetic to denounce Tito and his communists. In the end, they dearly paid for their passivity. The shortsightedness of the West also contributed to Tito's victory. In his interesting study, Charles Zalar states,

> By arming the partisan movement, by providing it with services of the BBC and the American Radio, by sending Allied officials into Yugoslavia and finally by cloaking this movement with its own enormous power and authority, Great Britain and the USA made themselves directly responsible for the rise of Tito to power[30].

---

30 Charles Zalar, *Yugoslav Communism: A Critical Study*. Prepared by the Subcommittee to investigate the administration of the Internal Security Act and other Internal Security Laws of the Committee on the Judiciary; 87th U.S. Congress, 1st Session, October 18, 1961 (Washington, D.C.: U.S. Government Printing Office), pp. 8-10.

Chapter III:
Dissidence and the Continuation of Titoism: 1945-1980

Introduction

The chaos of the civil war and the subsequent rise of Tito to power in Yugoslavia had considerable repercussions on the post-war character of the newly reestablished state. Yugoslavs who were suspected by the communist authorities as former Ustashi or Chetniks were sentenced to death. Those who did not lend sufficient support to the new regime, such as Christians or Moslems, were sentenced to high prison terms. Even those Yugoslavs who openly professed Catholicism, Croatian nationalism or anti-communism were officially identified as adhering to some non-communist faction of the civil war. Thus, many Croatian dissidents were often charged with "fascism," even though their age clearly precluded any ties with the former Ustashi. Similar was the fate of dissenting Yugoslav communists, who were often discredited as "Cominformists;" although, there seemed to be no evidence of their ties to Moscow. Chapter III illustrates the atmosphere of the Titoist terror in post-war Yugoslavia by presenting a wide variety of cases of well-known Yugoslav dissidents.

Purges and Persecutions: 1945-1948

One of the salient features of a communist regime's social construction of reality is its recurrent reference to the "heroic struggle" which facilitated that regime's ascendancy to power. Marxist tenets to which revolutionaries referred during their "underground" period gradually fade away and are replaced by post-war mythologies. Typically, the personalities of Marx and Engels became eclipsed by the cult of a new leader and an array of new heroes. After World War I, for example, the Soviets successfully combined the Marxist theory of class struggle with their guerilla warfare. The storming of the Winter Palace became in the collective memory of the Bolsheviks far more important than the Marxist theory of surplus value. Following World War II, the myth of the Winter Palace became supplanted by the myth of The Great Patriotic War for the socialist Motherland.

Communist mythology in Yugoslavia underwent the same transformation[1]. After World War II, the Marxist ideology became narrated to Yugoslavs through numerous stories and anecdotes of the partisans' cunning and courage. Minor partisan campaigns against the Germans, Ustashi or Chetniks were elevated to the level of major offensives which invariably carried Tito's partisans to ingenious victories. In contrast, enemy forces were characterized as cowardly, sadistic and inapt[2].

To keep the legend of partisan valor alive in Yugoslavia Tito did not allow the enemy banners of Ustashi, Chetniks and Fascists to disappear. Indeed, Tito nurtured these words in the new communist environment as convenient labels to assign to real or fictitious enemies. During the post-war period Croatian dissidents, regardless of their political conviction, were often stigmatized at their trials as "Ustashi elements" by Titoist prosecutors. The old dichotomy of capitalist versus proletarian, which constitutes the essence of Marxist teaching, found its replacement in the new dichotomy of Ustashi or Chetnik versus partisan.

Tito masterfully applied this new revolutionary rhetoric to his opponents and at the same time benefited from the mutual distrust of the various ethnic groups. Every time Tito fabricated a Ustashi danger, he could count on gaining further support from even the most reticent anti-communist Serbs. After the war, when Serbs started complaining about the summary executions of captured Chetniks, Tito would then carry out executions against real or fictitious Ustashi elements; thus, diffusing Serbian opposition. For the majority of the Serbs, the choice seemed clear: Either put up with the ignominous Titoist regime or live in fear that some day revitalized Ustashi units might threaten Serbia.

The silencing of Croatian dissidents on charges of Ustashi sympathies went hand-in-hand with the excavation of Ustashi prison camps where the Ustashi allegedly massacred hundreds of thousands of innocent Serbs. One of

---

1 The adaptability of Marxist teaching to all spheres of life (history, art, mathematics, etc.) has brilliantly been described by Alexander Zinoviev, *Sans Illusions* (Paris: L'Age d'Homme, 1979), p. 33. "When one Soviet mathematician demonstrates his theorems, the other establishes the analogy between plus and minus and bourgeoisie and proletariat."

2 This is not only Dedijer's attitude, which was previously discussed, but is shared by some foreign authors. See Phyllis Auty, *Tito* (London: Longman, 1970) and the great admirer of Tito, Fitzroy Mac Lean, *The Heretic: Josip Broz Tito* (New York: Harper Brothers Publishers, 1957). On the other hand, radical Croatian nationalists and former Ustashi who live abroad often extoll the cunning and valor of Croatian soldiers fighting the Chetniks and communist partisans. See the article "Hrvatske Termopile," in *Ustasa* (Buenos Aires), IV trimestre, 1984).

these camps, Jasenovac, soon acquired the exaggerated reputation as the "Balkan Auschwitz," for it is alleged that 600,000 Serbs, Jews, Gypsies and Croats perished there under the Ustashi terror.

Those who rejoiced at Tito's "denazification" of Croatia were not only Tito's sympathizers, but pro-Chetnik supporters who saw in this program the partial fulfillment of their own desires. By constant use of the word "Ustashi," Tito managed to demoralize the Croatian population and impose guilt and frustration on the post-war generation: The alleged sins of the fathers were visited upon the sons. Those who publically professed their Croatian origin or affiliation often encountered serious troubles and were simply discredited as "Ustashi."

From 1945 to 1948 the fate of Croats was exceptionally difficult. Mass deportations, purges, "show trials" and exodus decimated the Croatian nation[3]. Tito's promised democracy turned into a bloody travesty; the remnants of statehood which Croats enjoyed in pre-war Yugoslavia were reduced to a fictitious republic designed after the Soviet pattern. The centralization of power in the Yugoslav state gained again the upper hand. During his pacification of Croatia and during the years following the war, Tito had the unanimous support of Serbs. As soon as Tito turned toward the radical Serbian elements, however, he was accused by Serbs of his Croatian background and of enacting a hidden, but well planned, revenge against the Serbs. There are few Serbs in Serbia willing to pardon Tito's extermination of the Chetniks and the capture of their leader, Draza Mihailovic. The situation was now reversed. Those who celebrated the capture of Mihailovic were not only the Titoists, but also the Croats who saw the Serbian danger reduced by Tito.

There is still widespread belief among Serbs that Tito did more in favor of the Croats, and that he unjustifiably sentenced General Draza Mihailovic to death. Wide segments of the Western public, including even some members of the American government, contend that the Chetniks were the allies of the British and Americans, despite the Allied abandonment of

---

3 The exact number of executed after the war is not known. According to Ljubo Sirc, *The Yugoslav Self-Management* (New York: St. Martin's Press, 1979), "in 1954-55 there was a prison population of 300,000 persons, providing a large number for the workforce," p. 31. According to official Yugoslav sources, by 1952 there were 52, 506 political prisoners in Yugoslavia. It could be assumed that the majority of the prisoners were of Croatian origin. Amnesty International (*Yugoslavia: Prisoners of Conscience*, 1982), p. 3.

Mihailovic during the last years of the war[4]. It is important to remember that the Chetniks were the first to initiate resistance to the Germans as well as the communists; it is also true that Croatia was supported by the Germans during the war. What is often overlooked, however, is that the Chetniks saw in Croatian separatism just as big a danger as in the German occupying forces or in the communist partisans. It has been demonstrated in Chapter II that the Chetnik movement was primarily a Serbian movement, and not Yugoslav as some scholars in the West argue[5].

Serbian opposition and dissidents have been persecuted by the Titoists only on one account – different political ideology (liberalism or anti-communism). In contrast, Croatian dissidents were charged by Titoists on two accounts – different political ideology (anti-communism, liberalism or fascism) and separatism (the dismemberment of Yugoslavia). This unequal treatment of Yugoslav dissidents, which was also reflected in the Penal Code (see Chapter V), must carefully be examined because it sets the stage for the understanding of Titoist Yugoslavia. To a certain extent Titoists tolerated ideological diversity within the communist movement (liberalism and leftism) because Titoism, itself, deviated from the Soviet line. However, as soon as the hints of separatism became suspected (including those who claimed to be communists) the only response Titoists had was the most severe repression. This was particularly the case with Croats and ethnic Albanians, for example, who were usually charged with fascism and separatism.

Given the harshness of Titoist laws, Croatian dissidents went through more hardship than Serbian dissidents. The Serbs (be they Chetniks, fascists or neo-liberals) never attempted to dismember Yugoslavia; the Croats (whether leftist, fascist or communist) always expressed, overtly or covertly, a desire for the autonomy of Croatia. Therefore, when Croatian dissidents were sentenced to prison, their terms were much longer (see Chapter 5, "Administration of Justice").

---

4 Truman posthumously awarded the Legion of Honor to Colonel Mihailovic, which is still resented by American Croats. See *Zajednicar* (Pittsburgh), February 6, 1985. Letter to the U.S. Congress.

5 The Hoover Archival Documentaries, *Patriot or Traitor: The Case of General Mihailovich* (Stanford: Hoover Institute Press, 1979) refers to Draza Mihailovich as a "Yugoslav." In the report of the Commission of Inquiry, Mihailovich "was appointed Minister of War by the *Yugoslav Government*"(underline added), p. 481.

The Trial of General Draza Mihailovic

On March 24, 1946 the Belgrade government announced that it had captured General Draza Mihailovic, the leader of the Chetnik resistance. During the trial Mihailovic was sentenced to death. Tito's decision to bring Mihailovic to trial was not motivated by Mihailovic's alleged collaboration with the Germans. Tito's likely intention was to get rid of a potential rival for power, and the most expeditious way to bring this about was to sentence him to death[6]. Mihailovic's trial not only served to eliminate Tito's competition, but to a certain extent it served to appease Croatian nationalists.

The show trial of Mihailovic was met with dismay in the United States. The American decision to intervene came late, and in the eyes of many Serbs, this lateness of response was interpreted as a sign of betrayal. The American legation in Belgrade delivered a note which said:

> As the Yugoslav authorities are no doubt aware, U.S. Army personnel in an Allied liaison capacity were attached to General Draza Mihailovic's headquarters during most of the period of his military acitivity. They must also be aware of the fact that many U.S. airmen were rescued and returned to Allied lines through the undaunted efforts of General Mihailovic's forces[7].

Tito ignored the American protest and made quick arrangements for the execution of Mihailovic. He also made sure that not a single word would leak out about the Chetnik rescue of American servicemen lest the Yugoslav population become more sympathetic to Mihailovic than the Titoist cause.

> During the course of 1944, many hundreds of Americans flying bombing missions into Romania were shot down over Yugoslavia. Of those that were shot down, more than 500 and perhaps as many as 600 were rescued by the forces of General Mihailovic[8].

Further evidence that the Chetniks did not collaborate with the Germans was later published in America by Serbian emigrees who fought along with Mihailovic. The Serbian emigrees presented the document of the reward offered by the German occupying forces for the capture of both Tito and Draza Mihailovic[9].

---

6 For a detailed discussion of Mihailovich's trial see Hoover Archival Documentaries, Ibid.

7 Ibid., p. 9.

8 Ibid., p. 11.

9 Ibid., Section photographs.

In their efforts to discredit Chetnik forces, Titoists brought to trial some captured German soldiers, including Gestapo Colonel Fuchs. The trial finally turned into a farce since no evidence of Chetnik collaboration with the Germans could be established:

> Gestapo Colonel Fuchs, when questioned about alleged collaboration between Mihailovic and the Gestapo, declined that the Gestapo had any connection with Gen. Mihailovic and considered him an enemy just as they considered Tito[10].

On June 17, 1946 Draza Mihailovic was sentenced to death. The reason that Tito did not give in to American pressure is clear enough: Yugoslavia enjoyed in those years the enormous protection of the Soviet Union because Yugoslavia became the first communist and also Stalinist state in the Eastern block.

The execution of Mihailovic greatly antagonized even the most moderate Serbs, who saw in this act an additional proof of the conspiracy against the Serbs by the Croatian-born Tito and the ungrateful Allies. The frustration of the Serbs was exacerbated by the fact that Tito had included among his high-ranking staff some former Ustashi or pro-Ustashi personalities. In the new Tito entourage there was a considerable number of former pro-fascist and pro-Ustashi Croats who now passionately supported their new master; for example:

1. General Franjo Pirc – a former commander of the Ustashi Corps in Croatia.

2. Antun Augustincic – Vice President of the Anti-Fascist Council of the Committee of National Liberation. He was an important sculptor in Croatia who before joining the partisans created a widely publicized bust of the Ustashi leader Ante Pavelic.

3. Vladimir Nazor – First President of Anti-Fascist Council of the Committee of National Liberation. For some time after the German occupation, Nazer functioned as a *poeta laureata* of the Croatian fascist press.

4. Colonel Marko Mesic – Commander of the Croatian volunteer units in the Soviet Union. His troops were among the first to enter Stalingrad in 1942. During his missions with German and Croatian troops, Mesic sent a telegram to Pavelic, informing him that the Croatian Legion ("The Devil Division") would fulfill their duty towards Croatia and Pavelic. After the

---

10 Dragnich, *Tito's Promised Land*, p. 25.

war and his captivity he became Tito's commander of the Guard of the Chief of State[11].

There is no doubt that these individuals were considered traitors to the Croatian cause, not only in the minds of Croats who fought with Pavelic (even when they realized they were losing the war), but also to Serbs. Examples of intellectuals or individuals switching from one faith to another abound in history and are not unique to Croats or any other nation:

> But since both communists and fascists have been brought to their ideological beliefs by motivations that are fundamentally psychological, the switch-over from one faith to the other presents no insuperable difficulties. The good communist makes a good fascist, and the good fascist makes a good communist[12].

It should be pointed out that many Ustashi might have been able to save their lives during the last months of the war had they defected to the partisans; however, the great majority of them remained faithful to their Croatian nationalism in the same fashion as Chetniks remained faithful to their Serbian nationalism. In his discussions with Croatian emigrants, the author was told that the Ustashi who defected to the partisans and were later captured by the Ustashi were treated in a more brutal manner than captured partisans.

People lacking courage to face historical data also lack courage to assume the responsibility for their own future and are often bound to create difficulties even for themselves. Not a single Serbian dissident, be he a liberal or conservative, publically denounced the Chetnik crimes in Eastern Bosnia and Hercegovina. Many Serbian dissidents also downplayed the partisan massacre of Croats at Bleiburg. Not a single Serbian dissident raised his voice, regardless of his love or hate of Titoism, against the discriminatory policies practiced by Titoists against Croats.

The resentments which Croats nurtured against Serbian supremacy and the King during the short life of the prewar monarchy, are still alive today and seem to be stronger than ever. Croats in the old Yugoslavia were under-represented in the army, police and government, the three crucial powers of the state. In communist Yugoslavia, Croats were again under-represented in the same institutions. Hoping that a nation would willingly participate in the founding of a state by virtue of slogans, such as "brotherhood and unity",

---

11 David Martin, *Ally Betrayed: The Uncensored Story of Tito and Mihailovich* (New York: Prentice Hall, Inc., 1946), pp. 121-128.

12 Ibid., p. 129.

without proportional representation in vital institutions is one form of self-delusion which can have disastrous consequences.

The Trial of Andrija Hebrang

The number of persecuted Yugoslavs, the plethora of citizens who became dissidents against their own will, was enormous. It would be an injustice to talk only about the hardships of one nation and forget the plight of the others. After the war, practically everyone was a potential target of the OZNA (the secret police later replaced by UDBA) even for such trivial reasons as "insufficient collaboration with the partisans" or by being a distant relative to some killed Ustashi or Chetnik. There are also numerous cases (which the author of this book knows from personal contacts) where neighbors, who for some reason could not get along before the war, saw the opportunity to denounce each other to the communist authorities and, thus, seemingly secure their peace in the following years[13].

Owing to its peculiar multi-national character, communist terror in Yugoslavia left deep scars on the entire population. Class hatred went hand-in-hand with national hatred. Early in 1946, influential communist leaders who were suspected of strong national ties or were lenient with dissidents also became the target of the OZNA. For the old communist partisan, the fact that he participated in the anti-fascist guerilla war was not a sufficient guarantee of being exempted from Titoist purges. Tito's desire to eliminate potential future leaders of Yugoslavia was strong, especially concerning communist leaders who might be better able to govern the state. By all means Tito's communist takeover and consolidation of power in Yugoslavia was ruthless; it was simultaneously directed against class enemies, national enemies, potential competitors and internal enemies (traitors, revisionists, and Trotskyites).

To what extent every revolution devours its own children can be examplified by the execution of Croatian communist leader and Tito's rival, Andrija Hebrang. Until 1945 Andrija Hebrang was one of the most influential leaders in the Yugoslav Popular Resistance (NOP). Hebrang's leadership in war-torn Croatia and Bosnia and Hercegovina, his relentless fight against the

---

13 The trend of mutual suspicion and denunciation continued until recently. Beginning in January, 1984, the Yugoslav government created 12,000 "regional committees," which urged Yugoslav citizens to call the telephone number 985 and report "counter-revolutionary activities." As reported in *Der Spiegel,* March 12, 1984, these government measures represented "a network of total control" ("*ein Spinnetz totaler Ueberwachung*").

Ustashi and Germans, is well known even among Serbs. During the war he was captured by the Ustashi and was kept in captivity briefly until he was released in exchange for captured Germans. The mere fact that Hebrang spent some time in Ustashi captivity was sufficient reason for Tito to accuse him of collaboration with the Ustashi and sentence him to death. Finally, Hebrang also was a Croat and for the Serbian-dominated OZNA that was enough of a crime.

Since actual evidence against Hebrang could not be collected and displayed it had to be fabricated by the Titoists. Informants were forced to testify against Hebrang; after which, they were also killed by the secret police[14]. In order to discredit Hebrang completely, the police pressured Hebrang's captured wife, Olga, to testify against her own husband. In his published documentary novel, Dr. Ivan Supek (one-time communist and today one of the most respected Croatian scientists and philosophers) relates the odious ordeal of Hebrang's wife during her confrontation with the general of the secret police:

> General – "Mrs. You heard in the papers about your husband. Sure, you know more about the whole case. No, no. I don't need your whole marital confession. We will be so considerate as to change your name and send you to live somewhere else. Just give us a couple of hints about your husband's treason."
>
> Olga – "I know nothing about all this."
>
> General – "Sure, but you can't deny, either, his ties with the Ustashi during his captivity."
>
> Olga – "This is not true!"
>
> General – Don't lie. This might get you in a very dangerous situation!"
>
> Olga – "General, for God's sake! I am Jewish. The Ustashi and Germans killed all my family and relatives. How could I live with one of their agents?"
>
> General – "Don't pretend to be a saint. Lujo Cacic told us everything. You were in bed with him."
>
> Olga – "Never!"[15]

Dr. Supek was well acquainted with Olga Hebrang, who must have given him valuable material about the brutality of the Yugoslav Secret Police.

This brief dialogue between Olga Hebrang and the OZNA general represents just a small glimpse into the state violence in Yugoslavia, which often went beyond imagination. In the West, hardly anyone took a firm stand in favor of the innocent victims. The fact that Titoists often described their victims as "fascists" was apparently sufficient motivation for democratic-minded Westerners to turn their heads away from Yugoslavia.

---

[14] See Ivan Supek, *Krunski svjedok protiv Hebranga* (Chicago: Markanton Press, 1983).

[15] Ibid., pp. 148-149.

Persecution of the Church

The persecution of the Church in Yugoslavia started immediately after the war and continued well into the following decades. Considering the variety of religions in Yugoslavia, the new communist government simultaneously persecuted the Catholic, the Christian Orthodox and the Muslim clergy. However, given the strong ties between the Croatian Catholic clergy and the Vatican, the cases against Catholics in Croatia are more fully documented than those which occured in Serbia and in some parts of Bosnia and Hercegovina. There is no doubt that the Islamic and the Orthodox faiths were under equal attack; yet, due to the lack of Islamic and Orthodox centers in the West there was also less outcry in Western capitals about their persecution. The communist persecution of religion was based on two motives. Politically, the communists saw in the church and its followers a rival capable of organizing the masses and, consequently, weakening the position of the new communist regime. Ideologically, religion was viewed by the Marxists as the "opium of the people" and, therefore, inconsistent with communist sensibilities in Yugoslavia.

The number of killed and imprisoned clergymen in Yugoslavia after the war has not been established. Yugoslav dissidents usually put the number of killed clergymen at three hundred, with at least twice as many imprisoned. The figures could be much higher, but due to the lack of evidence, these figures must remain purely hypothetical[16]. Regardless of the actual figures of persecuted clergymen, the activities and influences of the churches and mosques in Yugoslavia were greatly reduced.

The persecution of the church in Yugoslavia was carried out to a larger extent than in any other communist-ruled country in Eastern Europe. This can be partly explained by the events of the civil war in Yugoslavia which had a strong religious base. During the civil war, the Ustashi were not only fighting against the atheistic partisans, but were also actively involved in the persecution of the Orthodox Church and their adepts, who were predominantely Serbs. The same attitude prevailed among Serbian Chetniks who simultaneously persecuted Muslims, Croatian Catholics and atheistic communists. As a result of this, all leaders of the respective faiths were after the war charged with collaboration with the Ustashi, Germans or Chetniks by the Titoist regime[17].

---

[16] In a very objective book, Stella Alexander, *Church and State in Yugoslavia Since 1945* (Cambridge: Cambridge University Press, 1979) sets the number of Catholic priests at "243 dead, 169 in prison, 89 missing – total of 501", p. 70.

[17] Ibid., p. 170 and passim.

Even well after the war, communist Yugoslavia remained one of the rare Eastern European countries (unlike Poland or Czechoslovakia) where religious festivities were not publically celebrated and where an overt manifestation of religiosity was viewed by the state as a direct manifestation of ethnic nationalism. For all practical purposes, Christmas and Easter were not celebrated in Yugoslavia because the days celebrated as Christmas by the Catholics and the Orthodox are not the same. If the communist government had yielded to one group's celebration and not the others, this would have been interpreted as a direct insult to the other.

The Trial of Fr. Varnava Nastic

The case of the Serbian Orthodox priest, Varnava Nastic, is just one on the long list of new Christian martyrs. He was born in America where his Serbian-born parents had emigrated in the beginning of the century from Austrian-ruled Croatia. At the age of nine he returned to Yugoslavia, and when he became ordained he started his pastoral work in the Serbian-populated regions of Croatia. During World War II, he witnessed the hardships of the Orthodox Serbs who were relentlessly persecuted by the Ustashi. Pavelic pressed him to cooperate with the new Croatian government but Varnava refused. Varnava's staunch opposition to fascism and communism (or extremism of any kind) caused him a great deal of trouble from the various waring factions. After the war, he landed in a communist jail with the charge of "collaboration with fascism." Varnava was an exceptionally courageous man who dared challenge the Titoist authorities even when his fate was uncertain. During his trial, the public prosecutor asked him,

> "What is your attitude toward the Yugoslav Army?"
> "My attitude toward the army is the same as toward all armies."
> "We are not interested in your philosophical attitudes."
> "I don't live outside my philosophy. I express myself only philosophically"[18].

For his boldness and intellectual integrity, which the Titoists never tolerated, he was sentenced to eleven years of hard labor. Three years later he became injured in an accident with the railroad, where he was assigned to work together with his Croatian friend, Catholic bishop Peter Cule. He was later placed under house arrest and in 1964 died as a broken man.

---

[18] Ibid., p. 175.

The Trial of Cardinal Aloysius Stepinac

The trial of Catholic Cardinal Aloysius Stepinac was one of the most spectacular trials recorded in Eastern Europe, and because of its substantial publicity in the West, it is also one of the better known. Cardinal Stepinac was charged with "fascist collaboration and conspiracy against mankind" and, in accord with communist practice, he was condemned to death before his trial even started. Unfortunately for the Yugoslav authorities, no evidence of Stepinac's collaboration could be produced during the trial; consequently, the mock trial only tarnished the Yugoslav image in the West. The Cardinal turned from the accused into the accusor, revealing documents about the partisans which greatly embarrassed Tito and his government. The failure of the Stepinac trial led the Yugoslav communists to the decision to conduct further trials in secrecy[19].

Cardinal Stepinac was a symbol of the Catholic Church in Croatia as well as a symbol of national identity for Croats. For many Croats, he was both a spiritual and a political leader. It must be emphasized that, for Croats, Catholicism is not only a faith but it is above all a repository of their nationhood which they have managed to preserve during thirteen turbulent centuries. Catholicism has helped to preserve the whole nation from extinction. By putting Stepinac on trial the communist authorities in Yugoslavia hoped to reduce the nationalistic sentiment in Croatia once and for all, a sentiment which inevitably expresses itself through Catholicism.

Cardinal Stepinac was brought to trial in 1946 and charged as a collaborator with the Nazis and Ustashi. Despite numerious protests from abroad and a lack of evidence, Stepinac was sentenced to sixteen years of prison and subsequently placed under house arrest until he died in 1960. Many Croats at home and abroad, including a large number of Serbs, considered Cardinal Stepinac an uncompromising spokesman against both fascism and communism. This opinion is shared by some foreigners who, shortly after Stepinac's trial began, took a firm stand in favor of the Cardinal. For example, a speech given in 1946 by Louis Breier, late president of the American Jews, was printed in an issue of *Nova Hrvatska*:

> This great man was charged with collaboration with nazism. We Jews firmly deny that. We know from his past, and starting from 1943, that Stepinac was a true friend of Jews who suffered under Hitler's pogroms. He is one of the rare men who raised up against the Nazi

19 See the superbly documented book by Richard Pattee, *The Case of Cardinal Aloysius Stepinac* (Milwaukee: The Bruce Publishing Co., 1953).

tyranny in the times when it was dangerous. He spoke openly against the Nuremberg laws[20].

In his numerous pastoral letters and missives written to Ustashi leaders during the war, Stepinac criticized the arbitrary persecution of Serbs and Croats alike. In a letter to the Ustashi leader, Ante Pavelic, Stepinac complains about the treatment of the political prisoners in Ustashi-run camps and calls the camp of Jasenovac "a shameful stain on the honor of independent Croatia"[21].

The reason Stepinac received a harsh sentence had nothing to do with his alleged collaboration with Nazis; rather, his sentence was due to his bold and provocative statements against communism and the new Titoist government in Yugoslavia, statements which greatly irritated the court. During his trial, the Cardinal publically accused the communist court of duplicity and false moral judgements with the following words:

> I was not persona grata to either the Ustashi or Germans. I was not an Ustashi, nor did I take their oath as some of the officials of this court did, whom I can see here [underline added][22].

Stepinac was referring to those individuals who defected to the partisans during the last months of the war, who were previously fervent Ustashi members. The Cardinal raised other substantial issues as well:

> You accuse me as an enemy of the state and the people's authority. I acknowledge your authority. But what WAS my authority? I repeat again, you have been my authority since may 8, 1945, but not before that. Where is it possible in the world to obey two authorities; you in the woods, they (the Ustashi) in Zagreb?[23]

Stepinac's correspondance with the Ustashi officials and his speeches were never made public in Yugoslavia. His trial remained an issue which nobody in Yugoslavia was allowed to openly discuss. It can be argued that the primary purpose of sentencing Cardinal Stepinac to sixteen years in prison was to try to neutralize the Catholic Church, the traditional repository of Croatian nationalism. It was also a "routine" trial against any form of organized religion which the communists in Yugoslavia depicted, as "opium of the people," as a belief inconsistent with Marxism. The suppres-

---

20 Quoted in *Nova Hrvatska*, February 26, 1984.
21 Richard Pattee, Ibid., p. 103.
22 Ibid., p. 239.
23 Ibid., p. 240.

sion of leaders of powerful institutions in Yugoslavia by the new communist regime was probably based on political expediency and the desire to eliminate potential opposition to the new power of Titoism.

The Persecution of Former Comrades

Hannah Arendt demonstrates that totalitarian movements can never really constitute themselves as genuine political parties, but must continue to operate only as revolutionary movements[24]. The communist totalitarianism put in practice by Tito and his followers was never designed to solidify Yugoslavia by forging a consensus of the diverse nations and individuals of different political philosophies. When the real enemies were liquidated, new ones had to be found lest the revolution come to a stop.

In 1948, Titoist Yugoslavia was expelled from the COMINFORM and the Soviet Bloc. The expulsion was welcomed in the West, which perceived in it signs of democratization and the eventual shift toward democratic pluralism. Tito's subsequent crackdown on Stalinist dissidents in Yugoslavia fit in with the West's scheme of "rollback" of communism in Eastern Europe. In 1948, the Yugoslav prisons began filling up with new contingents of political prisoners. Side-by-side with German prisoners of war and alleged collaborators sat former partisan commissars who could not believe that Tito would betray them and their revolution. The first wave of persecution by the Titoists seemed to be subsiding, providing a little relief to the old dissidents. The second wave of persecution began smashing upon the Yugoslav Stalinists who now became dissidents, themselves. An old anti-communist prisoner and long-time friend of the author, recounts those days:

> From 1946 to 1948 we all thought at Nova Gradiska (a prison camp) that our sudden and inexplicable death was imminent. We were like walking corpses living on the installment plan with no will to resist and with no will to survive. What matters brushing teeth or going to the toilet if within two weeks you are no longer among the living.
>
> Then one night in October, 1948, we were startled with the arrival of familiar faces. Yes, faces of those who only two years ago sentenced us to death and long prison terms. Attorneys, prosecutors, generals, well-known partisans, here they were all heaped up in one cell with dozens of us. Stripped of their rank and uniforms, shaved to the skin, they suddenly appeared normal, sympathetic, and such was their behavior.
>
> Our situation dramatically improved; we were given better clothing, food, and above all, hope. The prison wards kept telling us that those people were traitors who wanted to kill Tito

---

24 Hannah Arendt, *The Origins of Totalitarianism*, pp. 341-388 and passim.

and the popular revolution. My sentence was reduced. Instead of serving eight years, I was released after four ..." (name withheld).

Arso Jovanovic, the legendary communist who initiated the revolution in Serbia was executed. Many young Yugoslavs later learned in school that Jovanovic was among the first to ignite the communist revolution, but few of them ever learned that he was also among the first to be devoured by the revolution. While the West was full of praise for Tito's new independent Yugoslavia, Tito was himself busy setting up new prison camps to house his old comrades-in-arms who remained faithful to Stalin's Soviet Union. Those who were not immediately executed were sent on an extended stay to Naked Island (*Goli Otok*) prison camp, which quickly became a notorious symbol for Tito's Gulag.

A New Generation of Dissidents: Milovan Djilas

Despite the widespread persecution and repression of all kinds of organized opposition the voices of dissidents in Yugoslavia could not be silenced. When dissidents ceased manifesting themselves among the ranks of non-communists, they nonetheless became active in the ranks of the Titoists. For Tito, to discredit his own communists as "revisionists," "liberals" or "imperialists" the task was more delicate and seemed barely convincing to his ardent supporters. Communist dissidents represented a far more dangerous threat because their activities were harder to control and they enjoyed a closer relationship and communication with Tito.

Among the high-ranking communists who openly rebuked Titoism and advocated parliamentary democracy in Yugoslavia was Tito's closest advisor and Vice-President of Yugoslavia, Milovan Djilas. Tito's relationship with Djilas, prior to the latter's conviction, was that of a father to a son.

Born in Montenegro of Serbian origin, Djilas remained until 1955 an undisputed leader in Yugoslavia and was honored together with Tito as a mastermind of the Yugoslav communist ascendency to power. In 1956 he was sentenced to prison for openly criticizing Tito and for publishing in the West his already well known book, *The New Class*.

During the war Djilas was in charge of partisan recruitment and the head of political propaganda. After the war, together with the head of the secret police Alexander Rankovic, Djilas was in charge of Tito's security and took an active part in the persecution of the Church, collaborators and

Stalinists[25]. He became a communist celebrity by plotting the execution of Andrija Hebrang and by his strict control of Croatian communists, whom he never trusted.

Although Djilas was often hailed in the West as a "Yugoslav Solzhenitsyn," it is important to understand that his name was widely ignored by Yugoslavs. Neither did Djilas enjoy a particular popularity among the Yugoslav dissident intellectuals, who often referred to him as a political chameleon, strongly responsible for the post-war repression. Croats in particular despise him. They often call him "Djilas the Croativore" (*Djilas Hrvatozder*); thus alluding to his obsessive hatred of a separate Croatia. During the war he was a dogmatic Stalinist committed to world revolution and never cared about political compromises as long as they furthered communism: Djilas became a more devoted Stalinist, accepting the purges as necessary and justifying the Nazi-Soviet Pact with all its ramifications[26].

Like many communist revolutionaries, Djilas (despite his meager education) maintained that a revolutionary should excell in all walks of life. He initiated an agrarian reform program in Yugoslavia which destroyed the traditional Yugoslav village and drove peasants into exile and prison. He changed the educational system, stripping the universities of outstanding professors and replacing them with half-educated Titoist commissars. Finally, he masterminded the notorious "self-management" program, the economically disastrous results of which are evident today.

There is no doubt that Djilas showed some honesty and moral courage in the last years of his vice-presidency, but he represents a typical case of the self-styled intellectual whose previous activities and policies served to damage Yugoslav unity rather than further it.

Signs of Thaw and New Repression: "Croatian Spring," 1971

A number of Western observers mistook Tito's policies of the de-Russification and de-Stalinization of Yugoslavia as genuine attempts to bring about de-communization. The well-publicized "decentralization" and "self-man-

---

[25] Djilas partly admits this in a series of articles published by *Der Spiegel*, "Der Rote Monarch," July 7 – August 4, 1980.

[26] Dennis Reinhartz, Milova Djilas: *A Revolutionary as a Writer* (New York: Columbia University Press, 1982).
It is interesting that the *Wall Street Journal, The Washington Post, The New York Times, Le Monde*, etc. often published Djilas's essays, while a few Croatian dissidents had the opportunity to appear in major European or American newspapers.

agement" led many to believe that a pluralistic Yugoslavia, compatible with Western standards, would be just a matter of time. The flourishing of the Yugoslav economy and massive departure of Yugoslav citizens to the Western countries in the middle 1960's was interpreted as a sign of positive change, confirming the Western prognosis of the gradual withering away of communism in Eastern Europe.

In 1966, Tito dismissed his friend and the head of the secret police, Alexander Rankovic, and the same year he initiated and promulgated a set of laws that was to set the stage for "democratic centralism." By the end of the 1960's a foreign tourist travelling in Yugoslavia must have been favorably impressed; there were tourist complexes, nude beaches, foreign cars driven by Yugoslavs, and so on. The scene must have appeared more like the capitalist West than a communist country.

The "liberalization process" also became translated on the ideological level. Yugoslavia witnessed in those years a curious phenomena: Side-by-side with the official Titoist-Marxists there was a "critical left", a situation unique in Eastern Europe, yet tolerated by the party[27]. Everything seemed at its best and Tito's communism appeared to be functioning well.

In 1969, Tito boasted that he had solved the national question in Yugoslavia. The year 1971 proved exactly the opposite. It became the most challenging year for Tito as well as the entire Communist League. Mass demonstrations and student riots proved that the Croatian question had not been solved. The Croatian people time and again demonstrated that Tito's Yugoslavia was not necessarily a Croatian Yugoslavia.

The "Croatian Spring" was for Tito truly embarrassing; this time it was not some "Ustashi" element trying to overthrow the government which was behind the Croatian national upheaval. It was his own comrades, party members of the Central Committee, who advocated more autonomy for Croatia and more independence in Yugoslav internal affairs. Most of the leading communists in Croatia maintained that they were only exercising their freedoms guaranteed by the constitution while simultaneously benefiting from the "liberalization" process initiated by Tito himself. Unlike other communist leaders, Tito had made a political mistake of great proportions by trying to impliment the constitution not only *de jure*, but also *de facto*, forgetting that this was not feasible in a totalitarian state where true national representation did not exist.

Croatian communists used the same logic that Tito once used against Stalin: Sovereignty of the state (in this case, of the Republic guaranteed by the constitution), but the maintenance of monolithic Marxist ideology. Tito

---

27 Called "Praxis," abolished in 1974.

was, thus, caught in his own trap, but in order to preserver the integrity of the state of Yugoslavia, he abandoned the "liberalization process" and returned Yugoslavia to the previous *status quo ante*. In December of 1971, Tito sent military police to Croatia, dismantled the Croatian Communist Party and charged them with "rotten liberalism, chauvinism and counter-revolution"[28]. His injunctions against the Croatian communists strangely echoed Stalin's words against Tito in 1948, only this time he did not mind using the same old Stalinist principle of repression.

Like his predecessor, Serbian King Alexander Karadjordjevic (1929), Tito was more concerned with the preservation of Yugoslavia than with ideological consistency. Coincidentally, the police orders (*ukaze*) issued against Croatia had been dispatched from Tito's estate, "Karadjordjevo", which had belonged to the former Yugoslav King. For Croats, the name of Tito's estate became a symbol of the anti-Croatian and pro-Serbian policies implemented by the Belgrade government. By mid-January, over 500 people had been arrested and the diminished Communist Party in Croatia was placed under strict surveillance by the UDBA[29]. As a result of the crack down, various publications were seized and banned, and many prominent intellectuals were forced into exile. Due to effective totalitarian controls put into practice by Tito, the "Croatian Spring" did not succeed, but it nevertheless left a clear message: Although nationalism may lay dormant, it was certainly not extinct.

Summary of Chapter III

This chapter has shown that the violence which characterized Yugoslavia during World War II continued in Yugoslavia after the war under Titoism. Tito successfully used police repression against real fascist collaborators as well as fictitious ones. Often, as in the case of the persecuted Yugoslav clergy, Titoist violence was directed against democratically minded persons who were equally opposed to fascist and communist totalitarianism.

During his power-consolidation phase, Tito succeeded in removing some of his closest communist friends. It is interesting to observe that the violence which occured among communist leaders was not unusual. Purges initiated by communists against dissenting communists often occured in newly-established communist states.

---

28 Gruenwald, *The Yugoslav Search for Man*, p. 56.
29 Ibid., pp. 56-57.

Despite his crack-down on all forms of opposition, Tito did not succeed in his most difficult task: the suppression of nationalism in Yugoslavia. The events which occured in Croatia in December 1971 proved that Titoism had its shortcomings and that Yugoslavia's unity was not strong. As a consequence, Tito adopted a firmer policy for the control of potential dissidents in order to preserve his power and the unity of Yugoslavia.

The following chapter will discuss how Titoists controlled Yugoslav emigrants and dissidents who lived under the jurisdiction of foreign countries. It will be seen that Titoists employed methods against emigrant dissidents which were often more brutal than those applied at home.

Chapter IV:
"Open Borders" and the Secret War Against Yugoslav Emigrants

Introduction

In contrast to Chapter III, which discussed the persecution of Yugoslav dissidents in Yugoslavia, Chapter IV will deal with Titoist persecution of Yugoslav dissidents living abroad. Much has been written about Eastern-European secret police operations in Western Europe. According to prominent Soviet defectors, the KGB (in cooperation with other Eastern-European secret police organizations) carried out extensive activities in the West. It is suspected that the assassination attempt of Pope John Paul II was masterminded by the Bulgarian secret police and the Soviet KGB[1]. In his interesting book, *Terror and Communist Politics*, Robert Adelman discusses at length the role of the secret police organizations in Eastern Europe and provides some salient information about their inconspicuous terror network in the West[2]. It must be observed that very little has been published so far about the Yugoslav secret police (the UDBA) and its war against exiled Yugoslav emigrants. In contrast, much more is known about real and alleged cases of terrorism of Yugoslav (primarily Croatian) emigrants against communist Yugoslavia.

This chapter will document some cases of suspected UDBA assassinations of Yugoslav emigrants which occured in Western countries and which, up until today, have not been completely solved. Also, some cases of Croatian terrorism will be briefly described which took place both in the West and in Yugoslavia.

Tito's "Open Border" Policy

Tito's policy of opening Yugoslavia's borders, initiated in the early 1960's, resulted in immediate and practical changes for a large number of Yugoslavs. Many Yugoslavs settled in Western European countries, improved their material conditions, and contributed to the overall growth of the Yugoslav economy. The remittances of Yugoslav workers living and working

---

1 See "The Andropov Suspicion," *The Economist*, December 11, 1982.

2 Robert Adelman, *Terror and Communist Politics: The Role of the Secret Police in Communist States* (Boulder and London: Westview Press, 1984).

in Western, capitalist countries represented an important contribution to the Yugoslav budget and, consequently, contributed significantly to the pattern of development in Yugoslavia, erratic as it may have been[3]. Viewed in its entirety, the new "open border" policy had a three-fold result:

1. It considerably relieved Yugoslavia of the problems associated with the growing number of unemployed and those potentially unemployed.

2. It assured the constant influx of guest-worker remittances into Yugoslavia (hard currencies), which in turn helped the government create new jobs for domestic Yugoslavs.

3. Politically, the policy reduced the pressures of social and economic discontent, strikes and demonstrations, while at the same time curbing the rise of potential Yugoslav dissidents.

The effects of these new policies were spectacular. Hundreds of thousands of Yugoslavs from all regions of Yugoslavia travelled to Western countries, and after working there for several years, returned to Yugoslavia with new-found affluence. Due to the relatively decentralized Yugoslavia and the significant role of the private sector, the returning Yugoslav "guest workers" were often praised by the government as new job creators[4].

Yugoslav authorities usually described "guest workers" as temporary workers, although the temporary work for the majority of Yugoslavs lasted longer than ten years. Officially, the government showed great concern about Yugoslav workers leaving the country, while in reality it never opposed their departure to the West.

The great majority of Yugoslav "guest workers" were not politically active during their sojourn in the West. Part of this can be explained by the fact that many workers had relatives remaining in Yugoslavia; workers were afraid of reprisals against their families. Also, Yugoslavs traditionally tended to equate economic welfare with political freedom. All things considered, for many Yugoslavs working or living in the West, the new job they held served as an economic springboard which raised their material well being and boosted their social prestige when they returned to Yugoslavia. Not all "guest workers" returned to Yugoslavia; the number who remained in Western countries was truly enormous. Over one million Yugoslavs born

---

[3] How the Yugoslav economy worked under "self-management" is very well described by Ljubo Sirc, *The Yugoslav Economy Under Self-Management* (New York: St. Martin's Press, 1979).

[4] Returning "guest-workers" often complained about the Yugoslav government's heavy taxation, bureaucracy and the resentment which they encountered among Yugoslavs who remained at home.

in Yugoslavia after the war remained to live abroad as foreign citizens or temporary workers who were likely to become foreign citizens.

Among the economic emigrants who began leaving Yugoslavia in the early 1960's, a sizable number were motivated by the desire to continue their political struggle against Titoism in the more politically tolerant environments offered by Western democracies. Western states provided Yugoslav emigrants with the possibility to engage in the struggle against Titoism and the Yugoslav communist government so long as their activities were not detrimental to the Western state security. The emigrants' intention was to gain the attention of the influential politicians in the West and the media in order to induce them to be more critical with regards to Yugoslavia.

With the development of Yugoslav dissidence abroad, the Titoist government was faced with a two-fold enemy: One internal and relatively easy to deal with, and the other external, more committed, dangerous and difficult to silence. Yet, despite the new possibilities open to political emigrants, they were remarkably unsuccessful. Before engaging in the propaganda war against Titoist Yugoslavia, the dissident emigrants all too often conducted, a propaganda war against each other, a war reflecting national animosities. The real benificiaries of these propaganda wars were, as usual, the Titoist government and the Yugoslav Secret Police, the UDBA.

Croats constituted the majority of the political emigrants and therefore posed the greatest threat to Titoist Yugoslavia. Emigrant political activity among Croatian "guest workers" increased over time to the point that the Yugoslav government imposed stricter controls on the workers returning to Yugoslavia. Tito's "open border" policy had its immediate benefits to the state, but it also had its political liabilities.

Yugoslav Counter-Measures Against Emigrants

To prevent Yugoslav emigrants from getting organized into political factions hostile to Yugoslavia, Titoist authorities used all available means including psychological warfare, kidnapping and assassinations carried out by the Yugoslav secret police. In his interesting interview with the German-based *Der Spiegel*, Colonel Kaddafi of Lybia stated:

> Tito sent to the Federal Republic [of Germany] his hirelings to liquidate Croatian opponents. And yet Tito's prestige in Germany has not suffered in the least. Why should only Tito be free to do it and not me ...[5].

---

5 *Der Spiegel*, July 21, 1980.

Kaddafi's statement provides just a hint of UDBA illegal activities which were rampant in Europe, and West Germany in particular, during the '60s and '70s. UDBA dirty tricks increased over time in proportion to the increase of new Yugoslav emigrants. UDBA behavior against Croatian dissidents in the West hardly differed from that in Yugoslavia. All Croatian dissidents were invariably characterized as Ustashi, fascist or, interestingly, agents of the American Central Intelligence Agency (CIA). The primary purpose of UDBA was to discredit the image of Yugoslav dissidents abroad and enhance the image of Titoist Yugoslavia in the eyes of Western observers. Table #2 gives the names, which according to Rullmann, were killed by the UDBA[6]. Given the difficulties of documenting secret service assassinations, Rullmann's evidence of UDBA involvement in the murders he discusses is quite substantial, but it is always possible that the UDBA may not have been involved in every case.

In their secret war against Yugoslav emigrants, the UDBA often used the following tactics. Every assassination of a political opponent in the West was preceeded and followed by propaganda stirring up the quarrels and disputes between different factions of the emigrants. Usually, the UDBA first disseminated pamphlets with violently anti-communist and anti-Titoist texts in which the activities of moderate emigrants were sharply criticized and attacked as pro-Titoist[7]. It is instructive to observe that the UDBA seldom carried out an operation against a radical emigrant, but instead looked for its victims among moderately critical individuals who enjoyed considerable credibility in the Western states. Once the victim was kidnapped or killed, the responsibility for the act was placed on some other Yugoslav emigrant organization, or on the victim himself, accused of being a UDBA agent.

Allegations that Yugoslav dissidents abroad were carrying out a war against each other became widespread over two decades and led Western governments to assume that the UDBA was not actually involved in these crimes. Consequently, European governments were reluctant to step in and thoroughly investigate and control UDBA assassinations and abductions. In many cases, UDBA informants successfully infiltrated emigrant groups and with radical anti-Yugoslav rhetoric succeeded in discrediting emigrant activities.

6 See the very well documented book on UDBA assassinations by Hans Peter Rullmann, *Assassinations Commissioned by Belgrade* (Hamburg: Ost-Dienst Verlag, 1981, pp. 27-72). This is probably the only book of its kind published in the West.

7 Ibid., p. 13.

Table 2
List of Yugoslav Emigrants Allegedly Killed by the UDBA

1. Dr. Ivo Protulipac, Croat
2. Drago Jilek, Croat
3. Ilija Abramović, Croat
4. Dinka Domaćinović, Croat
5. Mijo Lijić, Croat
6. Nikola Martinović, Croat
7. Ivo Bogdan, Croat
8. Geza Pašti, Croat
9. Marijan Šimundić, Croat
10. Mate Miličević, Croat
11. Mile Jelić, Croat
12. Petar Tominac, Croat
13. Vlado Murat, Croat
14. Andjelko Pernar, Croat
15. Hrvoje Ursa, Croat
16. Djuro Kokić, Croat
17. Mile Rukavina, Croat
18. Krešimir Tolj, Croat
19. Vid Maričić, Croat
20. Nediljko Mrkonjić, Croat
21. Ante Znaor, Croat
22. Josip Krtalić, Croat
23. Mirko Ćurić, Croat
24. Nahid Kulenović, Croat
25. "Maks" Luburić, Croat
26. Josip Senić, Croat
27. Mirko Simić, Croat
28. Maksimir Krstulović, Croat
29. Stjepan Ševo, Croat
30. Tatjana Ševo, Croat
31. Rosemarie Bahrić, Croat
32. Pero Čović, Croat
33. Josip Buljan-Mikulić,Croat
34. Mate Jozak, Croat
35. Nikola Penava, Croat
36. Matko Bradarić, Croat
37. Stipe Mikulić, Croat
38. Ivan Tuksor, Croat
39. Ilija Vučić, Croat
40. Ivica Miošević, Croat
41. Zvonimir Kučar, Croat
42. Bruno Bušić, Croat
43. Ante Cikoja, Croat
44. Jozo Míloš, Croat
45. Križan Brkić, Croat
46. Mario Rudela, Croat
47. Zvonko Štimac, Croat
48. Goran Šečer, Croat
49. Cvjetko Cicvarić, Croat
50. Mate Milčević, Croat
51. Nikola Miličević, Croat
52. Jozo Oreč, Croat
53. Stanko Nižić, Croat
54. Antun Kostić, Croat
55. Mate Kolić, Croat
56. Ivo Furlić, Croat

1. Siniša Ocokoljić, Serb
2. Andrija Lončarić, Serb
3. Sava Cubrilović, Serb
4. Jakša Ljotić, Serb
5. Ratko Obradović, Serb
6. Petar Blagojević, Serb
7. Petar Valić, Serb
8. Miodrag Bošković, Serb
9. Mirko Stanojević, Serb
10. Dragiša Kašiković, Serb
11. Berisav Vasiljević, Serb
12. Dušan Sedlar, Serb

1. Vehbi Ibrahimi, Albanian
2. Barhosh Gervalla, Albanian
3. Jusuf Gervalla, Albanian
4. Zeka Kadri, Albanian

Source: Hans Peter Rullmann, Assassinations Commissioned by Belgrade, pp. 72, 73, 74

More important, however, was the result: There grew a pervasive fear that among the ranks of the emigrants there may be an UDBA informant or agent. This internationalization of "Udbaphobia" often prevailed over the fact of whether or not an actual informant existed in the group. There was no escape from the fears created by totalitarian regimes. Thus, a system of mutual fear becomes salient. On the one hand, the "Ustashophobia" of the Titoists led them to suspect every Croatian as a potential Ustashi "cutthroat", and on the other hand, the "Udbaphobia" of the exiled emigrant Croats led them to perceive in every newly arrived outspoken Croat a potential UDBA "hit man:"

> In this way UDBA sowed distrust among the emigrant ranks with the result it had hoped for, that UDBA, itself, was not incriminated with the murders committed. The hypothesis that the Croats were killing each other in the course of "internal disputes" was maintained for a long time by the German police until it had to be completely abandoned. Even the Serbs and the Croats, who were by no means friends with each other, even in exile, prefer to ignore each other rather than harm each other[8]

In August, 1967, in the center of Stuttgart, fatal shots were fired at the Yugoslav Consul, Sava Milovanovic. The perpetrator of the crime was a Croatian emigrant by the name of Franjo Goreta. The Yugoslav propaganda machine found exactly what it had looked for: Proof that Croatian emigrants were all involved in terrorist activities. Unfortunately, for the Yugoslav authorities, during his trial in Germany Goreta testified that he had been for some time an UDBA agent, himself. In his story he revealed that in Yugoslavia he had been forced to work for the UDBA and spy on Croatian emigrants. He also revealed that his station chief was Milovanovic, himself, who the day before the assassination, had given him the names of four emigrant Croats who were to be killed. He later declared in the court, "I had to kill him to save the others"[9]. Goreta was known to be the first UDBA defector who revealed the activities of his former employers to the German authorities. Goreta, who remained free in Germany, received several threats from the UDBA[10].

In order to better conceal its assassinations in the West, the UDBA occasionally recruited foreigners who were devoid of any emotional or ideological ties with the potential victim. This method represented less of a risk for the UDBA. For example, in 1967 the UDBA carried out the assassination of Marijan Simundic, a politically active Croat in West Germany, by hiring

8 Ibid., p. 13.
9 Ibid., p. 23.
10 Ibid., p. 24.

Brunhilde Koblenz (alias, Doris Andres) a native of Germany. One day Doris "accidently" encountered Simundic and asked him for a ride in his car. When she later told him to stop, shots were fired into Simundic from behind, presumably by an UDBA assassin. Doris managed to escape to Yugoslavia where, after some time, she became a Yugoslav citizen[11].

During the same year, two prominent Croats, Andjelo Pernar and Vlado Murat, mysteriously encountered fatal accidents at their place of work. Their deaths were never explained[12]. In 1968, Croatian emigrant Hrvoje Ursa was found dead in the Fulda River in West Germany[13]. One month after Ursa's death, three other Croatian emigrants were shot dead, among them a survivor from Bleiburg, Mile Rukavina, whom the West German government had earlier refused to hand over despite Yugoslav demands. German police found in the pool of blood, side-by-side with Rukavina, Kresimir Tolj and Vid Marecic[14].

Apart from the occasional assassination, Yugoslav authorities constantly harrassed Yugoslav travellers and "guest workers" returning to Yugoslavia[15]. For example, several years later when Vinko Tolj, the brother of Kresimir Tolj (mentioned above), returned to Yugoslavia after visiting the tomb of his dead brother in Germany, he was welcomed back by the Titoists with an unpleasant surprise: Ten years in prison for having layed a wreath at his fallen brother's grave. Between 1971 and 1978, alone, 320 Croatian "guest workers" had been sentenced with heavy penalties by Yugoslav courts upon their return to Yugoslavia[16].

Activities of the UDBA in Europe were extensive and complex. Through "Yugoslav clubs," various tourist agencies, and schools fully accredited by host governments, UDBA agents recruited informants, spied upon and closely controlled the activities of Yugoslav emigrants and "guest workers" in host countries. The children of Yugoslav "guest workers" were often obliged to register at Yugoslav schools (*jugoskole*) in Western Europe where they learned more about communist propaganda than they did about their own language[17].

---

11 Brunhilde Koblenz returned to Germany in 1983 and was immediately arrested. According to *Nova Hrvatska*, February 10, 1985 she was sentenced in Germany to nine years of prison.

12 Rullmann, p. 30.

13 Ibid., p. 31.

14 Ibid., p. 31.

15 This was often the case with each Yugoslav "guest-worker" who returned to Yugoslavia. See Rullmann, p. 32.

16 Ibid., p. 32.

17 *Neue Bildpost*, January 20, 1985.

Despite occasional protests by Western European governments, the spree of UDBA assassinations against Croatian and Serbian emigrants did not decrease. In March, 1969, a Serbian emigrant and former Yugoslav staff officer named Loncarevic was found dead in his Paris apartment. During the war, he collaborated with the Chetniks and the Allies and received many prominent awards from the British and French governments. The mystery surrounding his death has never been cleared, although many Serbian emigrants suspect the UDBA of the assassination[18].

The same year, in December, assassins forced their way into the apartment of Serbian emigrant Sava Cubrilovic who was living in Sweden. Shortly after he was murdured, the assassin, Milan Djokic, was detected by the Swedish police. Unfortunately, the warrant for his arrest was issued seventeen minutes before he boarded an airplane for Belgrade. The Swedish magazine *Fib-Aktuell* reported that the assassin was an agent of the UDBA[19].

In 1974, UDBA assassins entered the apartment of a prominent Serbian emigrant intellectual, Ljotic, and shot him to death. Ljotic had been an important opponent of Titoism and, after the arrival of Solzhenitsyn in Europe in 1973, publically vowed that he would write about Tito's Gulag in the same way Solzhenitsyn wrote about the Soviet Gulag[20].

In 1978, a spokesman for the Croatian National Council, Bruno Busic, was shot dead in Paris while leaving his friend's apartment. Busic was probably the most prominent Croatian exiled dissident, and his premature death is still considered a great loss to Croatia. His intellectual prestige, broad culture and, above all, the credibility he enjoyed among Western politicians gained him considerable respect even among traditionally hostile Serbian emigrants. During 1971, he was one of the intellectual leaders of the "Croatian Spring" and, after Tito's crackdown on Croatian dissidents in December of the same year, he was forced to flee from Yugoslavia on a forged passport. After his assassination, the Serbian emigrant newspaper, Iskra, reported:

> All the indications point towards the fact that the assassination of Busic was carried out by the UDBA. If one considers ... the ruthless reign of terror of the UDBA over political emigrants, then one should show more solidarity, irrespective of political differences of opinion[21].

---

[18] Rullmann, p. 36.
[19] Ibid., p. 36.
[20] Ibid., p. 37.
[21] Quoted in Rullmann, p. 63.

Although some Croatians have been involved in terrorist activities, including the assassination of Yugoslav diplomats, their activities were more extensively reported than UDBA activities. It is important to observe that Croatian terrorism was mostly based in Western countries and, for a variety of reasons, did not manifest itself very often in Yugoslavia. Due to logistical problems and the totalitarian nature of the Yugoslav regime, Croatian terrorist activities in Yugoslavia did not bear any fruit and were quickly detected by the Yugoslav authorities.

Like all other communist countries, Yugoslavia endorsed "armed struggle" so long as its goal was to overthrow "capitalist, fascist or colonial" governments. According to Marxist doctrine, terrorism is a necessary stage in the proletarian struggle against its class oppressors; in the case of the Titoists, terrorism was a major vehicle which facilitated their ascent to power[22]. Tito, himself, spent two years in prison in monarchical Yugoslavia for terrorism. Yugoslavia, as a leader of the "non-aligned" countries, actively promoted the "legitimate revolutionary and national rights of the oppressed people"[23]. Yugoslavia maintained excellent diplomatic relations with Kaddafi's Lybia and the Palestine Liberation Organization and supported many governments which in the West were depicted as "terrorist havens."

Yugoslav emigrants often pointed out Yugoslavia's connections with international terrorism and its support for governments which actively sponsor international terrorism. In one instance a Lebanese merchant ship with contraband (Soviet-made surface-to-air missiles from Palestinian sources) hid from the Italian coast guard in Yugoslavia's territorial waters. In another instance, the Italian police investigating Red Brigade terrorism accused Zoran Grbelj, a Yugoslav citizen, of complicity in the assassination of Francesco Coca, Italy's top public prosecutor. Grbelj declined to return to Italy or furnish any statement against the Red Brigades[24]. Yugoslavia also

---

22 Marx and Engels called it euphemistically "dictatorship of the proletariat." Trotsky, while still in power, wrote, "The man who repudiates terrorism repudiates also measures of supression and intimidation toward determined and armed counterrevolution. The man who repudiates the dictatorship of the proletariat, repudiates the Socialist revolution and digs the grave of Socialism," Leon Trotsky, *Terrorism and Communism* (Ann Arbor: The University of Michigan Press, 1961), p. 23.

23 Which includes the logistical and moral support of various guerilla movements; for example, the Algerian movement of independence from 1955-1962 and support of Mugabe's and Nkomo's guerillas during the war of independence from 1970-1977.

24 Gruenwald, *The Yugoslav Search for Man*, p. 312.

transferred a considerable quantity of Western-made military equipment to the Palestine Liberation Organization and other Marxist movements.

All this indicates that Soviet friends were also Yugoslav friends and that the Yugoslav "non-aligned" foreign policy was actually strongly in line with Soviet foreign policy. Yugoslavia was also a known sponsor of various nationalistic movements in the Third World and was among the first of the "non-aligned" nations to vehemently advocate the right of struggle for national independence, except, of course, when it came to Croatia. In the words of one important dissident interviewed by Dusko Doder after the Croatian Spring, "If Upper Volta can be independent, why not Croatia"[25]?

Today, most foreign observers generally agree that international terrorism was sponsored by the communist countries and usually financed by funds obtained from the Soviet KGB[26].

Many influential American and European authors and observers greatly misunderstood the nature of Croatian terrorism. A prominent American scholar, Robert Kupperman, wrote: "Since the end of World War II ... the Soviet Union has been the principal backer of the exile Croatian separatist movement, primarily to create problems for the Yugoslavian government under Marshall Tito"[27]. Kupperman's statement is very general and cannot be substantiated with any facts or evidence – neither does the author provide any in his book. In view of the previous description of the links between the Yugoslav goverment and other Marxist guerilla movements in the world, which were also backed by the Soviet Union, it can be concluded that, contrary to Kupperman, the Soviet KGB and the Yugoslav UDBA probably worked, hand-in-hand, or at least did not get in each other's way.

Sometimes Soviet newspapers showed great concern with the rise of Yugoslav emigrant activity in the West and, as usual, placed the blame on the American Central Intelligence Agency. In the communist party newspaper, Krasnaya Zvezda (Red Star), the Tass correspondent wrote that "the USA hides notorious fascist criminals, among them a good number of Ustashi and Chetnik terrorists. The USA gave sanctuary to a Chetnik Djuic who lives today in Chicago and is a head of a terrorist organization *Ravna Gora*"[28]. There is no evidence that Croatian extremists were financed by the KGB or any other Eastern European government. An overwhelming number of Croatian emigrants, despite their occasionally unreal nationalistic aspira-

---

25 Dusko Doder, *The Yugoslavs* (New York: Random House, 1978), p. 21.

26 See, Ray S. Cline, *Terrorism: The Soviet Connection* (New York: Crane Russak, 1984).

27 Robert Kupperman, *Terrorism: Threat, Reality, Response* (Stanford: Hoover Institute Press, 1979), p. 339.

28 *Krasnaya Zvezda*, December 27, 1983.

tions, considered themselves strong anti-communists and perceived Titoist Yugoslavia as an offspring of Soviet communism.

Among the few cases of Croatian terrorism which occured in the West, there are some which deserve special attention, mostly because they have never been fully elucidated. In February, 1971 Yugoslav security agents reportedly succeeded in inducing their Croatian adversaries into occupying the Yugoslav consulate in Göteborg, Sweden, in order to extort the release of Mijenko Hrkac, who had previously been sentenced to death in Yugoslavia for terrorism. It remains a mystery whether Hrkac was in reality an undercover agent working for the UDBA. The Croatian extremists eventually killed Yugoslav Ambassador Rolovic, a former communist general believed to have a blood-stained past in the service of the UDBA[29]. A year later, in September of 1972, a band of Croatian extremists hijacked a Swedish jetliner and demanded the release of their comrades involved in the assassination of Rolovic. The Swedish government gave in to the demands and released the extremists who subsequently found refuge in Spain[30].

In 1977, a group of Croatian extremists hijacked a Trans World Airline jetliner on a flight from New York to Chicago. In an elaborately planned affair involving five people, the hijackers took a "hoax bomb" onto the jetliner, while placing a real bomb in a baggage locker at New York's Grand Central Railroad Station. The extremists forced the jetliner to land in New Foundland, in Iceland and in Northern Europe. After landing in Paris, French security forces shot the tires flat on the jetliner and forced the hijackers to surrender. In the meantime, the real bomb placed in New York's Grand Central Station was removed; but a police officer was killed trying to detonate the device. Croatian extremists got what they wanted: widespread publicity in all the major international media[31].

Croatian Terrorism In Yugoslavia

Only one major Croatian terrorist operation occured in Yugoslavia, but due to its seriousness and duration it was reported in all Western media. As noted earlier, Tito was engaged in massive purges against Croatian nationalists in 1972, including a purge of the Croatian Central Committee. In the

29 See Jacob Sundberg's article in *International Terrorism in the Contemporary World*, ed., Marius H. Livingston with Lee Bruce Kress and Marie G. Waneck (Westport, Connecticut: Greenwood Press, 1978), p. 114.

30 Ibid., p. 114.

31 Edgar O'Ballance, *Language of Violence* (San Rafael: Presidio Press, 1979), p. 114.

aftermath of the purges a group of exiled Croatian extremists, members of the Croatian Revolutionary Fraternity (founded in Australia in 1962) decided to launch a suicide attack against communist installations in Yugoslavia in order to draw the attention of the world to the unresolved Croatian question. Nineteen heavily-armed Croatian extremists from all parts of the world met in Austria in 1972. They clandestinly crossed the Yugoslav border at Maribor, hijacked a truck and drove it all the way down to Hercegovina, a region known for its strong Croatian sentiments and presumed by the extremists as the most appropriate place for their armed struggle against the Titoists. This same region was once the hotbed of Tito's partisan guerillas; its difficult access, rugged mountains and network of bad roads provided an excellent hideout for the extremists. The Croatian extremists then attacked a police station, blew up two bridges, and finally retreated deep into the mountains[32].

The next day Tito dispatched 30,000 troops, territorial units, twelve helicopters, and members of the UDBA. The surrounding villages were sealed off, the roads were cut, and villagers were subjected to strict surveillance. The terrorist's incursion had a particularly bad effect on Yugoslav tourism, which became sharply curtailed due to the stricter controls placed on border crossings and foreign visitors wanting to travel to the Adriatic Coast that summer. On July 2, the Yugoslav media reported that the extremists had been smashed. Then three weeks elapsed and not a single word leaked out about the extremists. On July 13, the telephone communications lines connecting Belgrade with Sarajevo, the capital of Bosnia and Hercegovina, were cut for two days. Presumably, this was sabotage carried out by the Croatian extremists.

If and how the Croatian terrorists were captured has never been made public. The Yugoslav media showed the captured weapons, but never the captured extremists. It is possible, as *Der Spiegel* reports, that they were secretly trailed and sentenced to death on the spot by the Yugoslav authorities[33]. On the other hand, the wife of one of the extremists, Kathrin Andric who lives in Strassbourg, told *Der Spiegel* after the terrorist incursion was made public that, "eleven of the Croatian fighters are still alive, but nobody knows where they live"[34]. Probably the only ones who know were the Yugoslav authorities who were involved.

---

32 *Der Spiegel*, July 31, 1972.

33 Ibid.

34 Ibid.

Map 2
Croatian Extremists Incursion into Yugoslavia – 1972

Source: Christophe Dolbeau; La Croatie, 1990.

UDBA Assassinations Overseas

In the mid-1970's the UDBA stepped up its activities against Yugoslav emigrants living in the USA, Canada, Australia and New Zealand. The methods it employed were similar, if not more brutal, than those described above. In a speech given in the US House of Representatives in October, 1976, Congressman Philip M. Crane of Illinois drew attentions to Tito's campaign of terror with these words: "In the area of terrorism, of the brutal elimination of critics of the regime and the total government power, Tito's government is in no major respect different from other Communist governments'"[35].

Based upon subsequent UDBA activities, it appears that the Yugoslav government was not in the least moved or deterred by the rising voice of Western criticism of Yugoslavia's criminal policy in the West. On June 19, 1977 a Serbian exiled dissident and associate editor of the weekly journal *Liberty*, Dragisa Kasikovic, was found dead in his Chicago apartment together with his murdered nine-year-old step-daughter[36]. In January 1978, a Serbian emigrant and editor of *Liberty*, Mihailo Naumovic, mysteriously died in an automobile accident, falling from a bridge into the Chicago River[37]. The same year, a prominent Croatian dissident, Krizan Brkic, fell victim to UDBA bullets in Glendale, California[38].

In 1977 UDBA machinery appeared in South Africa, a country where nobody expected to see it, least of all its victim, Croatian Jozo Orec. Orec first went to Australia in 1961; after which, he moved to West Germany where he served four years in prison for alleged ties with the Croatian Revolutionary Fraternity (which in 1972 had made its incursion into Yugoslavia). After being released, he withdrew completely into family life in South Africa. Orec was killed, presumably by the UDBA, in the most sadistic manner. The assassins set him on fire, chopped off his head, wrapped the remains in a blanket, and threw it aside a road near Johannesburg. It appears that Orec was betrayed by his own countryman, Pavlic, an UDBA agent. Pavlic left South Africa and was reported to be living in Yugoslavia in the small city of Djurdjenovac[39].

UDBA crimes committed after the death of Tito clearly demonstrate that, despite protests by various Western governments, Yugoslavia's silencing of its external adversaries became part of its foreign policy. Part of the blame

---

35 Quoted in Gruenwald, *The Yugoslav Search for Man*, p. 282.

36 Ibid., p. 282.

37 Ibid., p. 282.

38 Ibid., p. 282.

39 Rullmann, pp. 59-60.

is also to be placed on the various Yugoslav emigrant organizations which often conducted debilitating campaigns against one another. Nobody could realistically expect that any Western government would pay more attention to one emigrant group than to another, especially given the fact that each emigrant organization claimed to represent the legitimate rights of their respective nation in the state of Yugoslavia. With such a fragmented emigrant situation, Western governments could never fully detect and fight against UDBA criminal activities; consequently, they fell into the trap of Titoist "anti-fascist propaganda," which (as seen) manifested itself through the indiscriminate killing of exiled Yugoslavs.

Summary of Chapter IV

The purpose of Chapter IV was to describe how Titoist Yugoslavia and its secret police dealt with Yugoslav dissidents who found refuge in Western countries. Given the fact that many Yugoslavs left Yugoslavia and began anti-Titoist propaganda in the West, it is understandable that the UDBA resorted to sending, under the auspicies of their diplomatic missions, its assassins to silence the dissidents.

The following chapter is somewhat different from previous chapters. It deals with the description of events which occured in Yugoslavia after Tito's death in 1980; although, some of the described events do not follow in a chronological order. After a description of the events in ethnic-Albanian Kosovo, the reader will be introduced to the Yugoslav "administration of justice" in regard to dissidents. Thus, the reader will gain a clearer understanding of communist law and how Yugoslav dissidents were sentenced by Yugoslav courts.

Chapter V
Dissidence and the Continuation of Titoism after Tito

Introduction

The economic problems Yugoslavia faced during its last ten years served as strong stimuli to the rise of new political dissidence and its consequent repression by the Yugoslav authorities. One of the most important events which took place in Yugoslavia immediately after Tito's death was the uprising of ethnic Albanians in Kosovo and the violent repression which followed.

The purpose of this chapter is three-fold: The first section will examine the continuation of Titoist repression after Tito's death in the ethnic Albanian region of Kosovo. The second section will explain how the Yugoslav Constitution, Penal Code and legal procedures were used to prosecute Yugoslav dissidents. Finally, the chapter will close by presenting several salient cases of political persecution which occured in post-Tito Yugoslavia.

Tito's Heritage

The year 1980 began with two ominous signs: the Soviet invasion of nonaligned Afghanistan and the death of Josip Broz Tito, the non-aligned leader of Yugoslavia. These two events gave rise to the wildest speculation concerning Yugoslavia's future. The question often asked by Yugoslavs was: Now that Tito is dead, will Yugoslavia disintegrate under the centrifugal forces of nationalism, or will it be engulfed into the Soviet sphere of influence? With the passing of Tito all previous achievements, whether good or bad, seemed suddenly obsolete. The majority of Yugoslavs became aware that the living Tito was no longer there, and that with his death, his myth too, might as well expire.

The seriousness of Tito's departure was not fully understood in the West. The "leftist" monthly, *Le Monde Diplomatique*, known rather for its prestige than its objectivity, published an unrealistic and exuberant article under the title, "Tito's Exceptional Heritage." The author, Victor Fay, portrayed Yugoslavia in glowing terms, almost a eulogy, more likely to be found in the official Yugoslav press than in democratic France:

> Repression in Yugoslavia is rare and stops at the threshhold of private life. We are far from the forced deprivation of jobs and deportations which Soviet dissidents are subject to[1].

Simultaneously, the French daily, *Le Monde*, known for its sober and less ideological approach to world issues, published an article on Yugoslavia written by Henri Fesquet:

> And everybody knows, without admitting it, that the slandering campaigns against Cardinal Stepinac remain among the most troubled issues ... in the climate of persistent ethnic and religious hatred and repression[2].

The German *Der Spiegel* lucidly attempted to analyse Titoism and "after-Titoism." In an interview given to *Der Spiegel*, Yugoslav dissident Djilas openly stated that Yugoslavia is "rotting away and that the process of decay started a long time ago, even during Tito's life"[3].

The Albanian Question

The "rotting away" of Yugoslavia began to become manifest shortly after the death of Tito. On April 10, 1981, ethnic Albanian students rioted in the region of Kosovo and several days later the Yugoslav authorities proclaimed a state of emergency in Kosovo. Military and police units from all over Yugoslavia were dispatched to Kosovo and the region was made inaccessible to domestic and foreign journalists and observers.

Kosovo became in 1981 the "Irish question" of Serbia. The long forgotten (rather, long supressed) ethnic Albanian question thrust itself into the center of Yugoslav domestic policy. The tremendous increase in the ethnic Albanian population in Kosovo (numbering 1.7 million today) made even the most a-national communists in Yugoslavia concerned with the future ethnic composition of the state. Could any future Yugoslavia (literally,"Land of Southern Slavs") remain exclusively under the control of Slavs when ten percent of the population is already non-Slav?

Things seemed so much easier under Tito's leadership. Czechs, Russians, Germans and other ethnic minorities either faced deportation or forcible assimilation and often willingly mixed in with the Slavic masses, rarely making any reference to their ethnic heritage[4]. This time, however, the Kosovo

---

1 Victor Fay, "L'exceptionnel héritage de Tito," *Le Monde Diplomatique*, March 1980.

2 Henri Fesquet, "Les religions en Yougoslavie," *Le Monde* (Paris), February 21, 1980.

3 Milovan Djilas, "Dieses Modell fault vor sich hin," *Der Spiegel*, July 14, 1980.

4 Gruenwald, *The Yugoslav Search for Man*, p. 272.

Albanians, with their highest birth-rate in Europe, derived their political inspiration from over the border in Albania, proper. Albanian resistance to assimilation into the Slavic masses was understandable because of the proximity of Albania, which maintains strong cultural and national ties with the ethnic Albanians in the Yugoslav region of Kosovo.

Kosovo Albanians claimed that they were being wrongly accused of separatism by the central government in Belgrade, and that all they wanted was to raise the region of Kosovo, to the level of the socialist republics in Yugoslavia. They argued that smaller nations – Montenegrins, Slovens and Macedonians – were granted this privilege after World War II, and that the ethnic Albanians should also have their own republic[5]. To have granted Kosovo the status of a republic, so the Titoists reasoned, would be equal to the *de facto* creation of another Albania, this time within Yugoslavia's borders. This would have lead to a very complex situation in regard to an already existing and recognized Albania. For Albania, this would only serve as an opportunity to try and incorporate Kosovo into Albania on the basis of ethnic legitimacy.

Seen from the international perspective, the creation of a non-Slavic republic in Yugoslavia raises the question of whether Yugoslavia could be called exclusively "Slav." By refusing to grant Kosovo the status of a federated republic, Yugoslavia furnished proof that the concept of "federated and equal republics and nations" had been a pure fiction and that Yugoslavia was truly a highly-centralized state[6]. Consequently, by neglecting the legitimate rights of ethnic Albanians in Kosovo, Yugoslavia in fact neglected the rights of its own federated nations.

Few Kosovo Albanians were convinced by Serbian arguments that they enjoyed a higher standard of living and more freedom of movement in Yugoslavia than in super-totalitarian Albania under Enver Hoxa. Again, as with the Croats, it can be seen that national feelings among the ethnic Albanians seemed more powerful than all notions of class struggle.

The central government in Belgrade chose to pursue the option of "carrot and stick" vis-a-vis the ethnic Albanians in Kosovo: The policy of occasional appeasement was combined with brutal force. Massive imprisonments

---

5 The history and claims of the Kosovo Albanians are well described and documented in a book by Arshi Pipa and Sami Repishiti, *Studies on Kosovo* (New York: Colombia University Press, 1984).

6 Under the Yugoslav constitution, Kosovo was an "autonomous region" in the federated republic of Serbia and under the jurisdiction of Serbia.

and killings (allegedly about one thousand) of ethnic Albanians during 1981 bore their fruits[7].

> The government appears to hope that it can tranquilize Kosovo with a mixture of military control, quick trials for agitators, a shake up of personnel, symbolic gestures and psychological warfare against Enver Hoxa's regime. Such wishful thinking assumes that most of Yugoslavia's Albanians really prefer to remain in Yugoslavia which has done more for them than Tirana for its own subjects[8].

In the wake of the April demonstrations, Yugoslav communist propagandists launched a massive campaign against Enver Hoxa's Albania in an attempt to divert the attention of average Yugoslavs from the real causes of the Kosovo uprising. Yugoslav citizens could now read in their daily newspapers about the "Albanian Gulags, prison camps and the barbarian regime of Enver Hoxa." To many citizens, this type of criticism of communist Albania appeared very significant, but they also asked the question: "Why did we not hear about this before?" Never before had the Yugoslav press so openly criticized Albania, not even during the period of "diplomatic freeze" which lasted until the middle 1960's[9]. One might assume that Yugoslavia, by criticizing another communist state after a period of conspicuous silence, inadvertently admitted its own past and present failures. Yugoslavia's dispropotionate criticism of Albania generated precisely the opposite results of those intended by the authorities. Many Yugoslavs assumed that *mutatis mutandis* the Yugoslav communist system did not differ greatly from the Albanian system.

The claims for autonomy of the ethnic Albanians in Kosovo have never been so strong as they are today. The uprising in Kosovo demonstrates that Tito's dream of "withering nations" did not become true in Yugoslavia. The issue of ethnic Albanians which had been purposely forgotten by all Yugoslavs came into the limelight of Yugoslav domestic policy. Long denied as a nation, the ethnic Albanians felt justified in their demand for a separate republic and blamed Serbia for not recognizing them as a nation. In April of 1980 the *New York Times* wrote that "Albanians are the disposed of Yu-

7 *Kurier* (Vienna), April 17, 1981 reports that up to 1000 people may have been killed in riots.

8 Stevan K. Pavlowitch and Elez Biberaj, *The Albanian Problem in Yugoslavia: Two Views* (London: The Institute for the Study of Conflict, 1980), p. 16 (hereafter referred to as Biberaj).

9 In the aftermath of the Kosovo riots, the Yugoslav press attacked neighboring Albania, depicting it as the "most repressive country in Europe." See *Vjesnik* (Zagreb) and *Politika* (Beograd), May and June, 1981.

goslavia, the lowest paid workers, looked down upon ... and economically exploited by the Serbs[10].

The popular wisdom in Yugoslavia which depicted Serbs as the only true martyrs who suffered the terrible Croatian reprisals during World War II slowly changed in the light of events in Kosovo. Croatian national demands could always be discredited in Yugoslavia and to a certain extent in the West because Croats always enjoyed higher living standards than Serbs. As a consequence, the Croatian argument that Croatia was exploited by the Serbs lacked credibility both in the eyes of Yugoslav Serbs and Western observers who saw in Croatian nationalism a rudimentary form of "tribalism." Further, Croatian anti-Serbian campaigns during the Ustashi regime considerably crippled the image of Croats after the war. This time, however, the roles were reversed. The Albanians from Kosovo perceived themselves as culturally and economically exploited and pointed out that they had historically been persecuted and massacred by the Serbs[11].

Serbs made recourse to the same rhetoric against Kosovo Albanians which Croats used against the Serbs. It is interesting to note that Serbs often purported that Serbian historical rights were threatened in Kosovo (an idea which Serbs also advocate in Croatia) in the hope of finding Croatian allies against the Kosovo Albanians. In contrast, when Croats used rhetoric which alleged that Croatian historical rights were being menaced by Serbs in Croatia, they ran the risk of being discredited as "Ustashi." While it was punishable by law to criticize the overrepresentation of Serbs in diplomacy, party organs and the government, it was considered quite natural to criticize "primitive" Albanians who "should go back to where they came from." It appears that Serbian pro-Yugoslav standards were, officially, welcomed in Croatia, but not Albanian standards in Serbia.

It must be emphasized that anti-Titoist dissidents, apart from a few courageous individuals, did take a firm stand in favor of the Kosovo Albanians. Serbian intellectuals who were often hailed in the West for their liberal views did not publically denounce the killing of Albanians in Kosovo. One might also assume that Serbian dissidents could not reconcile themselves with the fact that Kosovo, an historical part of Serbia, today contains a majority of Albanians.

A paradox also emerged in relation to Croatian dissidents, many of whom supported the Albanian cause. Croats, who were so exuberant about their self-image and the image of "primitive Serbs", suddenly discovered the political virtues of Kosovo Albanians who were more successful in challeng-

---

10 Darton, "Tito's Yugoslavia," *The New York Times*, April 13, 1980.

11 Biberaj, *The Albanian Problem in Yugoslavia*, pp. 26-27.

ing the concept of Yugoslavia[12]. Croatian sympathy toward Albanians nevertheless remained dubious because Albanians are considered more "oriental" and "primitive" than Serbs, who are at least fellow Slavs. It can be concluded that Croatians felt more comfortable with the Kosovo Albanians because of their geographical distance and the similarity of their plight vis-a-vis the Serbs. Nevertheless, behind this game of intellectual duplicity and false moral appearances, the role of Yugoslav dissidents as a counterbalance to Titoism often turned into travesty.

Internal Security in Yugoslavia: Dissidents and the Administration of Justice

The Police

The enforcement of law in Yugoslavia was the responsibility of two state police organizations – the Direction of State Security (UDBA) and the Public Security Service (SJB). The SJB operated as a "people's militia" and was closely connected to the less conspicuous UDBA, whose priorities pertained to the detection, supression and repression of political dissidents. The UDBA represented the modern-day version of the OZNA, Tito's state security force founded in 1944 in the "liberated" territory of Yugoslavia. By the mid-1960's the UDBA changed its name into the SDB (State Security Service); although, the Yugoslav public continued to refer to it as the UDBA and its agents as "Udbasi."

The activities of both the UDBA and the SJB were supervised by the federal Secretariat of Internal Affairs in Belgrade. The Secretary of Internal Affairs was appointed by Tito, or by the Presidium after his death. The architect of the UDBA was Alexander Rankovic, a Serbian partisan and, until his ouster in 1966, a close advisor and friend of Tito[13]. After Tito's death the Secretary of Internal Affairs "rotated" every year according to the rules of self-management. Under the 1966 Basic Laws on Internal Affairs, the Federal Secretariat for Internal Affairs was responsible for coordinating and supervising the works of both police organizations; however, under Article 50 of the law, data and information concerning the internal organization and operation of the UDBA were considered the domain of official secrecy[14].

---

[12] Emigrant Croats and Albanians founded the "Croatian-Albanian Committee" which was very critical of communist Yugoslavia.

[13] Rankovic's funeral was attended by 100,000 Serbs in Belgrad. The event was not reported in the Yugoslav press. See *Encyclopaedia Britannica, 1984 Yearbook,* p. 732.

[14] Robert E. Bartos, "National Security" in Nyrop, *Yugoslavia: A Country Study*, p. 265.

In 1971, Yugoslavia ratified the two international United Nations treaties pertaining to human rights and committed itself to guaranteeing the rights of the freedom of opinion, expression, association and free speech. In 1978, Yugoslavia submitted a report on the implimentation of its policies in regard to human rights:

> The Socialist Federal Republic of Yugoslavia on the basis of the established objectives of its foreign policy relating to respect for the principles set forth in the Charter of the United Nations concerning the dignity of inalienable rights of men and women and respect for human rights an freedoms actively undertakes measures which ensure the protection of the civil rights recognized therein[15].

Yugoslavia also ratified the Convention on the Political Rights of Women and signed the Final Act of the Conference on Security and Cooperation in Europe (the 1975 Helsinki Accord).

Constitution, Penal Code and Human Rights

The Yugoslav constitution, enacted in 1974, guaranteed its citizens a number of fundamental freedoms and rights, including freedom of opinion, of the press, of assembly and speech, and confidential mail and telephone communications[16]. At first sight, the rights guaranteed by the 1974 constitution hardly differ from those enacted in the constitutions of West European countries. However, Article 203 of the Yugoslav Constitution explicitly stated that "No one may use the freedoms and rights established under the Constitution in order to disrupt the foundations of the socialist democratic order"[17]. Thus, the Yugoslav government, by assigning itself the privilege of interpreting "democratic order," put itself above all differing interpretations of "democratic order" and maintained the right to punish anybody for "undemocratic behavior."

The decision concerning what was democratic or undemocratic could be reached quite arbitrarily in Yugoslavia and offered no protection to a dissident for his legal defense. The indictment of dissidents was usually initiated by a public prosecutor who relied solely on the evidence of police agents. A number of dissidents reported that while being held without court protection (the police could hold suspects for three days before a judge investigated) they were subjected to psychological pressures, the extortion of false testi-

[15] Amnesty International Report, *Yugoslavia: Prisoners of Conscience*, p. 10.

[16] SFRJ, *Ustav*, 1974.

[17] Ibid.

monies and physical abuses[18]. In many cases, the accused were obliged to accept the services of a court-appointed lawyer[19].

In contrast to the Constitution, the Criminal Code was much more explicit and reflected the real nature of Titoist totalitarianism. Chapter Sixteen of the Criminal Code, concerned "Crimes against the Socialist self-managing system and Yugoslavia", stipulated the following:

> 1. Whoever, by means of an article, leaflet, drawing, speech or some other way, advocates or incites the overthrow of the working class and the working people, the unconstitutional alteration of the socialist social system of self-management, the disruption of brotherhood and unity, whoever maliciously and untruthfully portrays social-political conditions in the country shall be punished by imprisonment from one to ten years[20].

It can be seen from this article that the Yugoslav Communist Party alone could assume the leadership of the "working class" and that it skillfully protected itself from any criticism by naming it "malicious and untruthfully" portraying the social-political conditions in Yugoslavia. The same article also states: "Whoever commits an offense as mentioned in paragraph 1 of this article with or under influence from abroad shall be punished by imprisonment for at least 3 years"[21]. By "influence from abroad" the authorities typically referred to the capitalist West which, according to Marxism, represents the antithesis of the "working class." It can also be concluded that by punishing Yugoslavs returning from abroad, the Yugoslav authorities *de facto* condemned the very concept of Western democracy.

When the new Federal Criminal Code was introduced in 1976, the substance and the formulation of the corresponding articles remained unchanged. Article 118 of the Criminal Code virtually gave the authorities the opportunity to indict someone despite the lack of evidence that the person in question really committed any crime against the state. Article 118 speaks about "hostile" (*neprijateljska*) propaganda. *Neprijateljska* can be translated only very loosely and could mean in Croatian something pertaining to an "enemy" or "opponent". In convicting dissidents of various sorts of hostile propaganda or counter-revolutionary activities, the courts never took into consideration whether or not these activities had been carried out by violent means.

---

18 Amnesty International, Ibid., p. 24.

19 Ibid., p. 24.

20 SFRJ, *Krivicni Zakonik Jugoslavije*, article 133.

21 Ibid.

Sentences imposed for non-violent political offences were extremely harsh in Yugoslavia[22]. For those involved in terrorist activities there was hardly any possibility of appeal. If the terrorist activity resulted in the loss of life, the person was usually sentenced to death (see previous chapter, Miljenko Hrkac, a Croatian dissident). However, in comparison to the years after WW II, the punishment and the conditions in prisons seemed to be more humane. The ferocity of the camp Goli Otok was described by author Venko Markovski in *Island of Death*; he described the inhumane treatment of prisoners shortly after the war. Among the most notorious prisons in communist Yugoslavia where dissidents were detained, the following must be mentioned: Zenica, Foca, Stara Gradiska, Slavonska Pozega, Idrizovo, Nis, Zabela, Dob, and Sremska Mitrovica (see Map). According to dissidents, the conditions of Stara Gradiska were the worst; the camp was used by the Austrians, later by the Ustashi, and finally by the communists. It is reported that in Zabela, seventy-three inmates lived in a cell 6.6 m x 10.2 m or 19 x 30 feet; according to one dissident, "at rollcall at 5.30, all you hear is coughing"[23].

Under Article 63 of the Federal Criminal Code, a court could impose the security mesure of compulsory psychiatric treatment and confinement in a health institution on an offender who was not considered accountable for his acts. In 1978, a 29 year old Serbian student from Belgrade, Vladimir Markovic, visited Croatian dissident and former partisan general, Franjo Tudjman. During the discussion, Tudjman referred to the war crimes committed in Croatia by the Ustashi and showed that during his research he had come to the conclusion that the communist authorities had greatly exaggerated the numbers of Serbs killed by the Ustashi. Markovic was later indicted and confined to a mental insitution where he was declared to be suffering from a paranoid psychosis.

---

22 Amnesty International, Ibid., p. 27.

23 Ibid., p. 31.

Map 3
Prison Camps in Yugoslavia

1. "Lepoglava"
2. "Goli otok"
3. "Stara Gradiška"
4. "Sremska Mitrovica"
5. "Foca"
6. "Niš"

Source: Amnesty International: Prisoners of Conscience (London: A.I. Publications, 1982), p. 10.

Kosovo (Region)	221	prisoners
Croatia	210	prisoners
Bosnia & Hercegovina	194	prisoners
Montenegro	26	prisoners
Slovenia	54	prisoners
Macedonia	26	prisoners
Vojvodina (Region)	17	prisoners
Total Prisoners	910	

Toward The Total Control of Yugoslav Dissidents

The number of persecuted, imprisoned and killed Yugoslavs did not decrease in the years following Tito's death. According to reliable sources and testimonies provided by various emigrant organizations in the West, the total number of imprisoned Yugoslavs was even higher than during the two decades preceeding Tito's death. Amnesty International, the London-based human rights organization, maintains that the number of prisoners of conscience in Yugoslavia rose from approximately 300 in 1979 to 553 in 1980[24]. It must also be noted that during 1981, at least 2000 people were apprehended in the region of Kosovo, alone, and it is presumed that a large number of these Kosovars were held in Yugoslav prisons[25]. *Danica*, the Croatian-language weekly published in America (using sources from *Frankfurter Allgemeine Zeitung* and Amnesty International reports), puts the total number of imprisoned Yugoslavs at 910[26]: (see above)

Concerning the ratio of imprisoned to the number of inhabitants, the number of imprisoned ethnic-Albanians was the highest, with 13 prisoners per 100,000 inhabitants. Second on the list came the Croats, with 5 prisoners per 100,000 inhabitants. However, it must be kept in mind that the majority of prisoners of conscience in Bosnia and Hercegovina were of Croatian origin, which raises the ratio of imprisoned Croats to 9 prisoners per 100,000 inhabitants.

The rapid deterioration of the Yugoslav economy also accounted for a new surge of dissident activity. Yugoslavia faced an economic crisis of major proportion: Twenty-two billion dollars of foreign debt, approximately

---

24 Ibid., p. 29.

25 Pavlowitch, *The Albanian Problem in Yugoslavia*, p. 14.

26 *Danica* (Chicago), August 3, 1984.

one million unemployed, and an inflation rate of sixty percent[27]. Yugoslavia was at the top of the list of bankrupt Eastern European states. In previous decades, dissidence in Yugoslavia was motivated primarily by nationalism; during the eighties, many dissidents openly criticized Yugoslavia for the failure of its economic system and the increasing corruption among Yugoslav communist authorities. Arrests in Belgrade confirmed that the number of dissatisfied Yugoslavs was becoming larger and that in the eyes of many the legacy of Tito had become outmoded.

In February 1981, Croatian historian and former partisan general, Franjo Tudjman, was sentenced to three years of prison and five years of ban on public expression[28]. Tudjman had been at odds with the communist authorities ever since the late 1960's when he had left the Communist party. His firm criticism of the Titoist experiment and the concept of self-management resulted ina "show trial" in which he was charged with hostile propaganda and collaboration with the International Democratic Committee for Dissidents in Yugoslavia, which was based in New York. He was released from prison at the end of 1984.

The same year, another prominant Croatian, Dr. Marko Veselica (a former communist and son of a Yugoslav folk hero) was condemned to eleven years of prison. He was charged with hostile propaganda, incitement to national hatred, and conspiracy against the state[29]. A year before the charges were brought against him, he gave an interview to West German newspapers; the interview was reprinted in all major Yugoslav emigrant newspapers. Veselica was known for his criticism of the Yugoslav federation and his strong position in favor of an autonomous Croatia. Despite numerous protests from all over the world, Veselica went to prison.

In July 1983, Stjepan Djurekovic (former director of the largest Yugoslav petroleum corporation, the Zagreb-based INA) was found dead in Germany with his head hacked into pieces[30]. Several months prior to his death, Djurekovic had fled Yugoslavia and settled in West Germany where he demanded political asylum. Once in West Germany, he became active in revealing unpublished documents about Tito and the Titoists, many of whom he personally knew. His book, *Ja Josip Broz Tito*, was published in the West by Croatian emigrants. Apparently, due to the sensitivity of some of his published materials, the UDBA felt it necessary to step in and assassinate

---

27 *The New York Times*, September 19, November 27, 1984.

28 Amnesty International, Ibid., p. 14.

29 Ibid., pp. 40-41.

30 The series of articles by Hans Peter Rullmann in *Hrvatska Domovina* (Hamburg: Ost-Dienst Verlag, 1983), pp. 4-9.

him. Yugoslav authorities denied any responsibility. In the report on human rights in Yugoslavia published by the United States Department of State, allegations are made that Djurekovic might have fallen victim of another hostile emigrant organization[31]. This argument appears weak in light of other assassinations which happened in exactly the same manner and were directed against Yugoslav dissidents abroad. By reading the various emigrant publications, from the extreme right to the extreme left, it can be seen that Djurekovic enjoyed considerable popularity among all Croatian dissidents.

On April 20, 1984 the Yugoslav government took another step toward silencing Yugoslav dissidence. This time the victims were the Serbian liberal intellectuals who surrounded Milovan Djilas. In this action the UDBA apprehended twenty-eight people. This event was of particular importance because of the number of dissidents apprehended by the UDBA in one day[32]. The lawyer for the dissidents, the renowned Serb Srdja Popovic (also greatly respected by Croatian dissidents) was subjected to intimidation: His apartment was searched and several of his documents were seized. Due to the large publicity of the arrests in Western countries, the Yugoslav authorities were disposed to release all but three of the dissidents. On February 5, 1985, the *Washington Post* reported that Miodrag Milic, Milan Nikolic and Dragan Olujic were sentenced to two years, eighteen months, and one year, respectively. It should be noted that none of these dissidents directly attacked the foundations of "brotherhood and unity." Had they done that, like their counterparts from Croatia, their prison terms would have been much longer. The three dissidents based their criticism solely on the failure of self-management and the corruption of communist officials in Yugoslavia; consequently, a considerable number of Serbian communists were against the whole trial and made arrangements for the courtrooms to become accessible to Western observers.

In light of these events, it could be pointed out that Croatian prisoners of conscience fared far worse in the Yugoslav courts than their Serbian counterparts in Belgrade. In contrast to Serbian dissidents, both Tudjman and Veselica had superb revolutionary backgrounds, yet the Yugoslav press depicted them as traitors or pro-Ustashi criminals led by the American CIA. The Washington Post concluded that "sentences for three Serbian dissidents were softer than usual due to strong Western support for the defendants"[33].

---

31 U.S. Department of State, *Country Reports on Human Rights Practices for 1983* (Washington, D.C.: U.S. Government Printing Office, 1984), pp. 1171-1183.

32 *The New York Times*, July 16, 1984.

33 *The Washington Post*, February 5, 1984.

Summary and Conclusion

In light of the present chaos in ex-Yugoslavia many have called Titoism a necessary evil. The respect and fear which Tito instilled in his Yugoslav subjects had to do more with his policy of *divide et impera* than the true love of the people for their leader. Thus, the apparent paradox; Tito's adversaries rejoiced when Tito crushed the dissidents of a national faction perceived by the former as a worse threat.

Very often one hears in the West that Tito was after all loved by the entire Yugoslav population and that the majority stood firmly behind him. This is a preposterous overstatement, given the fact that all dictators, as Bainville remarks, "have to be adored and venerated by its citizens"[1]. History has irrefutably shown that the most sanguine dictators are usually those who benefit from the perfect consensus of their citizens. The love for Tito was carefully fabricated at the expense of each Yugoslav and, as noted earlier, was an active policy of Titoism. The excessive love for a dictator can easily turn into excessive hatred. Recent history demonstrates the best example. Djilas reveals that Tito could not understand why "the Chinese after Mao's death cooled off and ceased venerating the man who used to be their sole inspiration." Probably, Tito also anticipated that he might suffer the same historical fate once he departed.

All his life Tito wanted to substitute the notion of national struggle with the notion of class struggle. What happened in Yugoslavia was precisely the opposite. Forty years of Tito's iron rule could not eradicate nationalism in Yugoslavia, and similar attempts by his followers also failed. Had some other leader, even including a genuinely democratic leader, been head of the Yugoslav state the results of "Yugoslavization" would likely have been the same, but probably less painful.

Tito's followers in the former Yugoslavia are faced with an insurmountable obstacle: How to replace the ideology which went bankrupt in the East and which today mobilizes nobody in the West. To some degree, Titoism and non-aligned Yugoslavia were a last sanctuary for Western Marxists who saw in them an alternative to the rigidity of the Soviet system.

Many have argued that Yugoslavia was a good idea because it accommodated both the East and the West. Perhaps Yugoslavia was a good idea for

---

1 Jacques Bainville, *Dictators* (New York: Kennikat Press, Inc., 1967), pp. 261-262.

outsiders, but it was a tragic reality for its citizens and nations. The future of the war-torn Balkans looks grim, and one is reminded of the words of La Fontaine, who once said, *On ne croit au mal que lorsqu'il arrive* (We do not believe in Evil unless it happens).

Bibliography

Governmental and Institutional Publications and Documents

Amnesty International Report. *Yugoslavia: Prisoners of Conscience 1982.* London: Amnesty International Publications, 1982.

Encyclopaedia Britannica, 15th ed., s.v. *Yugoslavia.* Chicago: Encyclopaedia Britannica, Inc., 1983.

–: Book of The Year, 1984. *Yugoslavia.* Chicago: Encyclopaedia Britannica, Inc., 1984

–: Macropaedia, 15th ed. Chicago: Encyclopaedia Britannica, Inc., 1983.

The Hoover Archival Documentaries. *Patriot or Traitor: The Case of General Mihailovich.* Stanford: Hoover Institute Press, 1979.

Nyrop, Richard F., ed. U.S. Government as represented by the Secretary of the Army. *Yugoslavia: A Country Study.* Washington D.C.: Government Printing Office, 1982.

Pavlowitch, Stevan K. and Elez Biberaj. *The Albanian Problem in Yugoslavia.* London: The Institute for the Study of Conflict, 1981.

Sundberg, Jacob and Marius H. Livingston, ed. *International Terrorism in the Contemporary World.* Westport: Greenwood Press, 1978.

U.S. Congress, House Subcommittee to Investigate the Administration of the Internal Security Act, prepared by Charles Zalar: *Yugoslav Communism: A Critical Study.* 87th Congress, 1st Session, Oct. 18, 1961. Washington, D.C.: Government Printing Office, 1961.

U.S. Department of State. *Country Reports on Human Rights Practices for 1983.* Printed for the use of the Committee on Foreign Affairs and Foreign Relations of the House of Representatives and the Senate, respectively. Washington D.C.: Government Printing Office, 1983.

SFRJ. *Ustav.* Beograde: 1972.

SFRJ. *Krivicni Zakonik Jugoslavije.* Beograd: 1974.

Monographs

Adelman, Robert. *Terror and Communist Politics: The Role of the Secret Police.* Boulder and London: Westview Press, 1984.

Alexander, Stella. *Church and State in Yugoslavia Since 1945.* Cambridge: Cambridge University Press, 1979.

Arendt, Hannah. *The Origins of Totalitarianism*. New York: Harcourt Brace, Inc., 1955.

Auty, Phyllis. *Tito*. London: Longman, 1970.

Bainville, Jacques. *Dictators*. New York: Kennikat Press, 1967.

Berdyayev, Nikola. *The Origins of Russian Communism*. London: Geoffrey Bles, 1948.

Cline, Ray S. *Terrorism: The Soviet Connection*. New York: Crane Russak, 1984.

Curtis, Michael. *Totalitarianism*. New Brunswick: Transaction Books, 1980.

Dedijer, Vladimir. *Tito*. New York: Simon and Schuster, 1953.

Dedijer, Vladimir and Ekmecic, Milorad. *History of Yugoslavia*. New York: MacGraw Hill, Inc., 1974.

Djilas, Milovan. *Wartime*. New York: Harcourt Brace Jovanovich, 1977.

Doder, Dusko. *The Yugoslavs*. New York: Random House, 1978.

Dragnich, Alex. *Tito's Promised Land*. New Brunswick: Rutgers University Press, 1954.

Eterovich, Francis. *Croatia: Land, People, Culture*. Toronto: University of Toronto Press, 1964.

Faye, Guillaume. *Le Systeme à tuer les peuples*. Paris: Edition Copernic, 1981.

Fotich, Constantin. *The War We Lost*. New York: Viking Press, 1948.

Gruenwald, Oskar. *The Yugoslav Search for Man*. South Hadley: J.F. Bergin Publishers, 1983.

Jukic, Ilija. *The Fall of Yugoslavia*. New York: Harcourt Brace Jovanovich, 1974.

Kardelj, Edvard. *Sabrana Dela*. Beograd: Prosveta, 1981.

Kupperman, Robert. *Terrorism: Threat, Reality, Response*. Stanford: Hoover Institute Press, 1979.

Le Bon, Gustav. *La Révolution française et la psychologie des révolutions*. Paris: Gallimard, 1936.

Macek, Vladimir. *The Struggle for Freedom*. University Park: The Pennsylvania State University Press, 1948.

MacLean, Fitzroy. *The Heretic: Josip Broz Tito*. New York: Harper Brothers Publishers, 1957.

Martin, David. *Ally Betrayed: The Uncensored Story of Tito and Mihailovich*. New York: Prentice Hall, Inc., 1946.

O'Ballance, Edgar. *Language of Violence*. San Rafael: Presidio Press, 1979.

Pattee, Richard. *The Case of Cardinal Aloysius Stepinac*. Milwaukee: The Bruce Publishing Co., 1953.

Pipa, Arshi and Repishita Sami. *Studies on Kosovo*. New York: Columbia University Press, 1984.

Reinhartz, Dennis. *Milovan Djilas: A Revolutionary as Writer*. New York: Columbia University Press, 1981.
Rougier, Louis. *La Mystique Démocratique*. Paris: Edition Albatros, 1983.
Rullmann, Hans Peter. *Assassinations Commissioned by Belgrade*. Hamburg: Ost-Dienst Verlag, 1981.
Rusinow, Dennison. *The Yugoslav Experiment: 1948-1974*. Berkeley: University of California Press, 1977.
Sirc, Ljubo. *The Yugoslav Self-Management*. New York: St. Martin's Press, 1979.
Supek, Ivan. *Krunski svjedok protiv Hebranga*. Chicago: Markanton Press, 1983.
Trotsky, Leon. *Terrorism and Communism*. Ann Arbor: The University of Michigan Press, 1961.
Tudjman, Franjo. *Nationalism in Contemporary Europe*. New York: University of Columbia Press, 1982.
Zinoviev, Alexander. *Homo Sovieticus*. Lausanne: Diogenes Verlag, 1983.
–: *The Reality of Communism*. New York: Schocken Books, 1984.
–: *Sans Illusions*. Paris, L'Age d'Homme, 1979.

Newspapers

Krasnaya Zvezda (Moscow). December 27, 1983.
Kurier (Wien). April 17, 1981.
Le Monde (Paris). "Je suis mille fois plus responsable." November 14, 1984.
–: "Les religions en Yougoslavie." February 21, 1980.
Neue Bildpost (Hamburg). January 20, 1985.
The New York Times. "Tito's Yugoslavia." April 13, 1980.
Times (London). September 29, 1943.
–: "Tito has gone, terror survives." November 11, 1984.
Vjesnik (Zagreb) and *Politika* (Beograd). May through June, 1981, *passim*.
The Washington Post. February 5, 1985.

Periodicals

Danica (Chicago). "Porastao broj politickih progonjenika." August 3, 1983.
Djilas, Milovan. "Dieses Modell fault vor sich hin." *Der Spiegel*. July 14, 1980.
–: "Der Rote Monarch." *Der Spiegel*. July 7 - August 4, 1980.
The Economist. "The Andropov Suspicion." December 11, 1982.

Fay, Victor. "L'Exceptional héritage de Tito." *Le Monde Diplomatique*. March, 1980.
Hrvatska Domovina (Hamburg). "Stjepan Djurekovic." September, 1983.
Nova Hrvatska (London). "Zrtve Bleiburga." May 20, 1984.
Der Spiegel. "Vom Titokult zum Totenkult." May 12, 1980.
–: "So weit die Armeen kommen." September 10, 1984.
–: "Ein Spinnetz totaler Ueberwachung." March 12, 1984.
–: "Partisanen gegen Tito." July 31, 1972.
Ustasa (Buenos Aires). "Hrvatske Termopile." iv trimester, 1984.
Zajednicar (Pittsburgh). "Letter to the U.S. Congress." February 6, 1985.

EUROPÄISCHES FORUM

Band 1 Alexander Shtromas: Political Change and Social Development: The Case of the Soviet Union. 1981. 2. Aufl. 1990.

Band 2 Elisabeth Herrmann: Ecclesia in Re Publica. Die Entwicklung der Kirche von pseudostaatlicher zu staatlich inkorporierter Existenz. 1980.

Band 3 Alfred E. Ott/Nikolaus Wenturis (Hrsg.): Griechenland vor dem Beitritt in die Europäische Gemeinschaft. Beiträge des Symposions der Universität Tübingen in Verbindung mit dem Europa-Zentrum Tübingen vom 9. bis 11. Mai 1979. 1980.

Band 4 Michael de Ferdinandy: Die hispanischen Königsgesta. Portugiesische und spanische Geschichtsschreibung im Zeitalter der Renaissance. 1984.

Band 5 Inge Habig: Sich ein Bild machen. 'Bild' und ästhetisches Verhalten als System - eine Rahmentheorie für das Verstehen und Vermitteln von Kunst. 1982.

Band 6 William Otto Henderson: Manufactories in Germany. 1985.

Band 7 Hans-Erich Au: Die Strategische Verteidigungsinitiative (SDI). Zur politischen Diskussion in der BR Deutschland. 1988.

Band 8 Hans Filbinger / Heinz Karst (Hrsg.): Identität zur Zukunft der Deutschen. Klaus Hornung zum 65. Geburtstag. 1992.

Band 9 Volker Dreier: Zur Logik politikwissenschaftlicher Theorien. Eine metatheoretische Grundlegung zur Analyse der logischen Struktur politikwissenschaftlicher Theorien im Rahmen der Strukturalistischen Theorienkonzeption. 1993.

Band 10 Christoph E. Palmer: Der Bundestagswahlkampf 1986/1987. Eine systematische Darstellung der Wahlkampfführung der Bundestagsparteien und der Rahmenbedingungen der Wahl. 1993.

Band 11 Tomislav Sunic: Titoism and Dissidence. Studies in the History and Dissolution of Communist Yugoslavia. 1995.

Hans Filbinger / Heinz Karst (Hrsg.)

Identität und Zukunft der Deutschen

Klaus Hornung zum 65. Geburtstag

Frankfurt/M., Berlin, Bern, New York, Paris, Wien, 1992. 412 S.
Europäisches Forum. Herausgegeben von E. Ott. Bd. 8
ISBN 3-631-44939-9 br. DM 64.--*

Klaus Hornung lehrte Politikwissenschaft während der letzten dreißig Jahre in Reutlingen, Freiburg und Hohenheim. In dieser Zeit entstand ein umfangreiches wissenschaftliches Werk, besonders auf den Gebieten der internationalen Politik und Sicherheitspolitik, der politischen Ideengeschichte sowie der Theorie und Didaktik politischer Bildung. Im Sinn seiner akademischen Lehrer Hans Rothfels, Theodor Eschenburg und Arnold Bergstraesser hat der Jubilar seine Disziplin stets als "praktische Wissenschaft" verstanden und dementsprechend auch öffentlich in der politischen Bildung und Publizistik gewirkt. Die Überwindung der deutschen Teilung stand dabei immer im Vordergrund seiner Arbeit – auch in einer Zeit, als sie "nicht auf der Tagesordnung der Geschichte" zu stehen schien.

Die hier vorgelegten Beiträge angesehener Fachkollegen, von Freunden und Schülern spiegeln die Arbeitsgebiete und Wirkungsfelder von Klaus Hornung in einem breiten – auch internationalen – Spektrum wider.

Aus dem Inhalt: Das geschichtliche Erbe und die geistige und politische Lage der Deutschen nach dem Ende des totalitären Kommunismus und der Wiedergewinnung ihrer nationalen Freiheit · Deutschland und das internationale Konfliktfeld

Alexander Shtromas

Political Change and Social Development: The Case of the Soviet Union
2nd Edition

Frankfurt/M., Bern, New York, Paris. 1990. 173 pp.
Europäisches Forum. Edited by Prof. Dr. Klaus Hornung. Vol. 1
ISBN 3-631-42187-0 pb. DM 49.--*

A complex and tense relationship of «dissenting assent» between the various strata of the population of the USSR on the one hand, and the country's party state regime on the other is hidden under the monolithic surface of Soviet society. Its evolution spans the sixty odd years of the Soviet regime's continuing struggle against dissent. The future of the USSR and thus of the entire world will be affected by the course of this hidden confrontation. The effect of this situation on political change in the USSR is considered from a historical, sociological, and political perspective. Some general problems of political theory emerge from the discussion. Attempts are made at developing a general concept of political change. Models of such change are formulated and applied in consideration of future developments in the Soviet Union.

Contents: The Problem of Political Opposition in the USSR · The Soviet Regime and the Soviet People: an Historical Survey Present · Consensus and Dissent Political Change: Prospects, Ways, Consequences

Peter Lang Europäischer Verlag der Wissenschaften
Frankfurt a.M. • Berlin • Bern • New York • Paris • Wien
Auslieferung: Verlag Peter Lang AG, Jupiterstr. 15, CH-3000 Bern 15
Telefon (004131) 9411122, Telefax (004131) 9411131
- Preisänderungen vorbehalten - *inklusive Mehrwertsteuer